"Most 'kitchen books' are cookbooks, but not this one. *The Lazy Genius Kitchen* is your guide to strategic meal planning, organization, cooking, and cleaning up. You don't have to dread stepping into the kitchen, because Kendra Adachi shows you how to create a sustainable rhythm for managing your kitchen and feeding the people you care about. And you'll have fun doing it."

—JENNA FISCHER, actress, author, and producer/cohost of *Office Ladies* podcast

"Have a kitchen? You need this book. Kendra teaches you how to be the boss of your kitchen in all the ways that matter most to you."

—MYQUILLYN SMITH, *New York Times* bestselling author of *Welcome Home*

"Adachi is like the smart big sister I never had, revealing the secrets of a kitchen that not only take the stress out of daily meal prep, but actually make it fun. With warm, no-nonsense advice and proven formulas that liberate you from kitchen clutter and complicated recipes, *The Lazy Genius Kitchen* is an essential tool for living better every day."

—INGRID FETELL LEE, author of *Joyful*

"Whether you are a new cook in a quandary about getting something on the table over and over again each day or a seasoned professional who lives and works in the kitchen but gets weighed down by decision fatigue, Kendra is here to put a friendly hand on your shoulder and remind you what could and should really matter about keeping the heart of your household beating strong."

—BONNIE OHARA, author of *Bread Baking for Beginners* and owner of Alchemy Bread Co.

"This book is chock-full of smart cooking hacks, from tips to eliminating what you don't need to creating autopilot solutions that make it easier and more efficient to get meals on the table. I'm officially on the Lazy Genius cooking train. Choo choo, fellow food hackers."

—SHERRY PETERSIK, *New York Times* bestselling coauthor of *Lovable Livable Home*

"Having worked in restaurant kitchens, I understand that a well-organized kitchen is essential for speed, efficiency, and ease in cooking. Knowing that and living that are two completely different beasts. But Kendra empowers me to find and create systems that work for me. This is so much more than a system or a collection of rules. It's about embracing and loving who you are and working within that to create the space that works for you."

—ASHLEY RODRIGUEZ, creator of *Not Without Salt* and author of *Date Night In*

"Now that I have thought about how I can make my kitchen into a place that serves the needs and personality of my family, I feel empowered as I move through my daily kitchen chores. Kendra has shown me what matters . . . even a lazy cook like me."

—ANNA SALE, host of *Death, Sex & Money* podcast and author of *Let's Talk About Hard Things*

"I cook and talk about food for a living, and yet, there are weeks when I struggle to feed myself and my family the way I want to. What I love about *The Lazy Genius Kitchen* is that Kendra succinctly identifies and mutes the subconscious tape playing in our heads, the one that tells us all our meals have to check all the boxes simultaneously: healthy, quick, inexpensive, sustainable, Instagram-worthy . . . the list goes on. With Kendra's no-nonsense, witty, and practical advice, you'll feel empowered to choose your own priorities based on looking at your life with a kind, grateful eye. The result is not only empowerment but peace and gratitude even for the messy places. That's a skill I'll be using not only in the kitchen, but in the rest of my life, too."

—AARTI SEQUEIRA, cookbook author, chef, producer

The Lazy Genius Kitchen

HAVE WHAT YOU NEED, USE WHAT YOU HAVE, AND ENJOY IT LIKE NEVER BEFORE

KENDRA ADACHI

WATERBROOK

THE LAZY GENIUS KITCHEN
Copyright © 2022 by Kendra Joyner Adachi

All rights reserved.
Published in the United States by WaterBrook,
an imprint of Random House, a division of
Penguin Random House LLC.
waterbrookmultnomah.com

WATERBROOK® and its deer colophon are registered
trademarks of Penguin Random House LLC.

The author is represented by Alive Literary Agency,
www.aliveliterary.com

Library of Congress Cataloging-in-Publication Data
Names: Adachi, Kendra, author.
Title: The lazy genius kitchen: have what you need, use
what you have, and enjoy it like never before / Kendra
Adachi.
Description: Colorado Springs : WaterBrook [2022] |
Includes index.
Identifiers: LCCN 2021031552 | ISBN 9780525653943
(hardcover) | ISBN 9780525653950 (ebook)
Subjects: LCSH: Cooking. | LCGFT: Cookbooks.
Classification: LCC TX714 .A418 2022 | DDC 641.5—dc23
LC record: lccn.loc.gov/2021031552

ISBN 978-0-525-65394-3
Ebook ISBN 978-0-525-65395-0

Printed in Canada

9 8 7 6 5 4 3 2
FIRST EDITION

Illustrations and hand lettering by Sarah Horgan
Design by Marysarah Quinn

SPECIAL SALES Most WaterBrook books are available
at special quantity discounts when purchased in bulk
by corporations, organizations, and special-interest
groups. Custom imprinting or excerpting can also be
done to fit special needs. For information, please email
specialmarketscms@penguinrandomhouse.com.

This is not a cookbook.
This is a lifeline.

Contents

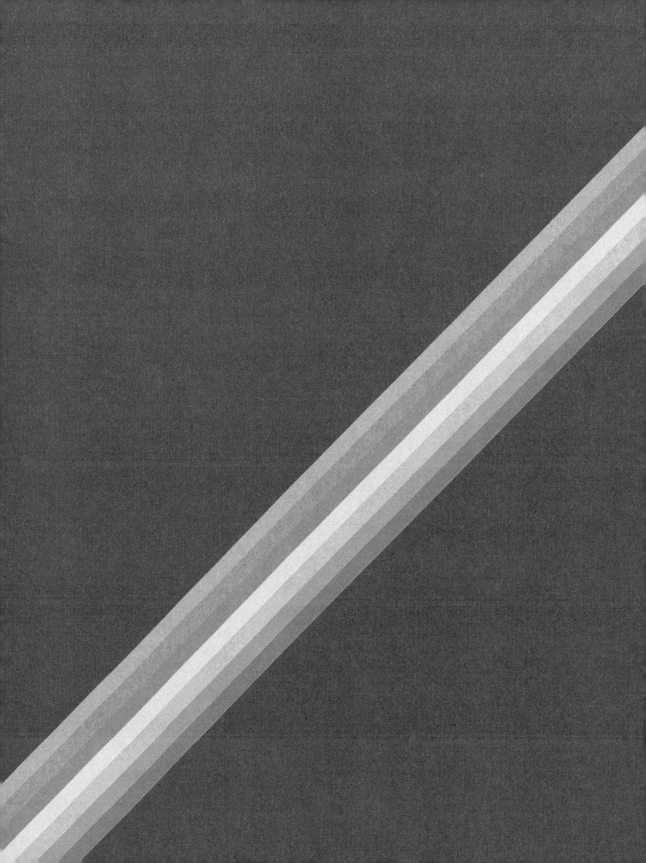

Lazy Genius 101

Hi! I'm Kendra. So nice to see you. Thank you for reading this book, but before you go any further, we need to cover something rather important. **You need to know what a Lazy Genius is.**

Obviously, you can't have a Lazy Genius kitchen without being a Lazy Genius, so here's your primer.

A Lazy Genius is a genius about the things that matter and lazy about the things that don't.

"Who decides what matters?" you ask.

You do.

You are the only person who can live your life, but my guess is you've been living that life according to other people's rules.

Ask me how I know.

As a self-help junkie, I spent years collecting tips and hacks, systems and manifestos, rules and routines to optimize my life. I spent countless hours and a ridiculous amount of mental energy building a big Machine of Life, trying to replicate the perfect day, succeed at the perfect goals, and be a generally perfect person.

However, that approach had its problems—namely, that I became more robot than human. Can you turn yourself into a cyborg? The jury's still out, but I say yes.

Living like a robot is living like a *genius*, and while genius sounds good in theory, it has its problems. You're at the mercy of everyone else's opinions, running yourself into the ground to live a perfect life. You're so obsessed with following a plan and doing it *right* that you ignore your own humanity.

Eventually, you hit a proverbial wall and simply can't do it anymore. My wall came in the form of motherhood, but walls aren't exclusive to life stage. We all hit one, and if you haven't yet, it's coming. Sorry to spoil your fun.

At that point—after all your genius plans dramatically fall apart— you swing to the other side of the spectrum and get *lazy*.

You give up on everything. You think, *If I can't do it perfectly, why do it at all? If I can't manage everything, why manage anything?* Enter being a "hot mess." The phrase is on all those t-shirts and coffee mugs for a reason. *It feels good.* However, working hard at being a mess is often just as draining as working hard to be perfect. You're a different-looking robot, but a robot all the same.

Listen, there's nothing wrong with order or with dirty hair and yoga pants. What *is* wrong is believing they're mutually exclusive. What *is* wrong is making snap judgments about a person, *including yourself*, about her value and vulnerability based on where she lands on the Lazy-to-Genius spectrum.

No one, and I mean no one, is completely together or completely a mess.

Being a Lazy Genius is not about either trying hard or giving up. Those don't have to be your only options. Which is rad, because you want to live a life that means something, right?

You want to invest your efforts in things that matter *to you.*

You want to feel secure when you walk in a room.

You want to be steady when things around you spin out of control.

You want to live a life of purpose and heart, connecting with your-self and the people you love.

You want to be yourself without bowing to everyone else's "shoulds."

Being a Lazy Genius is how you make that life happen. You're a genius about the things that *matter* and lazy about the things that *don't*.

And you get to decide what that is.

I got so jazzed about this idea a few years ago that I wrote a whole book about it.

It's called *The Lazy Genius Way: Embrace What Matters, Ditch What Doesn't, and Get Stuff Done*; it was a *New York Times* bestseller (which is not a crazy thing to say *at all*), and I truly believe it can make you more of who you already are *and* help you get stuff done.

Most self-help/productivity books give you a set of rules to follow based on what worked for the author. And I get that! When you love a new recipe or find an awesome kitchen gadget, you want to tell all your friends about this great new thing! But not everything works for everybody, no matter how good it is.

That's why *The Lazy Genius Way* is based on *principles*, not rules or systems you need to copy. These thirteen principles can Lazy Genius (yep, we made it a verb) literally *anything* based on what matters to *you*. You can slowly build a system, think strategically, and be intentional, all without being so daggum hard on yourself.

Here's a quick rundown of the principles if you're unfamiliar or just need a refresher.

These Lazy Genius Principles (LGP) are foundational, and I will refer to them throughout the book by their LGP number. You can always flip back here if you need a quick refresher.

Lazy Genius Principles

1. Decide Once
Limit your decisions by making certain choices once and then never again.

2. Start Small
Small steps are easy, easy steps that are sustainable, and sustainable steps actually go somewhere.

3. Ask the Magic Question
"What can I do now to make life easier later?"

4. Live in the Season
Welcome each season of life kindly and let it teach you something.

5. Build the Right Routine
The routine itself isn't what matters. It's simply an on-ramp to help prepare you for what does.

6. Set House Rules
House rules are about connection, not protection, and they prevent life from quickly getting out of hand.

7. Put Everything in Its Place
You don't have to become a minimalist; just put your stuff away.

8. Let People In
Invite people into your crisis, your celebrations, and all the ordinary in between.

9. Batch It
Do the same kind of task all at once.

10. Essentialize
Get rid of what doesn't matter.

11. Go in the Right Order
You already have the steps; you just need a better order.

12. Schedule Rest
Rest and self-care focus on doing what makes you feel like you.

13. Be Kind to Yourself
Value who you are now and without comparison to the past or the future.

Summarized from *The Lazy Genius Way* by Kendra Adachi (Colorado Springs: WaterBrook, 2020).

Congratulations! You've just completed the Lazy Genius crash course. If I had certificates, I'd give you one. Instead, I'll share a quick rundown of where we're going next.

How to Use This Book

The kitchen is so complex, is always in use, and feels way too big to figure out all at once. Besides, you've literally got dinner to make and can't waste your time on massive projects and meandering books.

That's why I broke this puppy down into parts and steps that actually work. Everything you need—and nothing you don't—all with the purpose of helping you have what you need, use what you have, and enjoy your kitchen like never before.

Part 1: **Your Lazy Genius Kitchen** is all about Lazy Geniusing all parts of your kitchen, using these five steps:

1. **prioritize:** name what matters

2. **essentialize:** get rid of what's in the way

3. **organize:** put everything in its place

4. **personalize:** feel like yourself

5. **systemize:** stay in the flow

Here, you'll learn the five-step framework that will transform your kitchen. You won't put anything into practice yet; it's all about getting the lay of the land.

I encourage you to read this part first and in order, because the right order *matters* (LGP #11). Going out of order is like listening to an album or playlist on shuffle; you'll enjoy the music, but you'll miss the magic.

Part 2: **Have What You Need** focuses on . . . wait for it . . . having what you need. But the point is not having what everyone needs, what I (Kendra) need, or what your favorite food blogger needs. It's about having what *you* need. I'll help you name what matters to you in six areas of your kitchen:

1. **space:** your actual kitchen + all the stuff inside it

2. **meals:** what you eat every day

3. **plan:** how + when you decide what to eat

4. **food:** choosing, storing + shopping for ingredients

5. **prep:** getting your kitchen ready for later

6. **table:** experiencing your meals

This is where you'll get practical and start applying the five steps from Part 1 to your kitchen.

Part 3: **Use What You Have** is a treasure trove of beautifully designed and supremely helpful resources so you feel equipped to enjoy your kitchen:

1. **techniques:** how to cook

2. **taste:** how to make food taste good

3. **tools:** how to use your stuff

4. **tasks:** how to keep up with it all

5. **tips:** how to make hard stuff easier

There's also a conclusion to remind you of the enjoyment that awaits you at the end of this journey, but it's short and sentimental rather than a list of steps. Life needs both, am I right?

These pages are full of Big Sister Energy, and I vow to be both excessively kind and helpful. I promise that these pages are a safe place, no matter your circumstances, personality, or skill set. I feel supremely confident—like, Beyoncé confident—that this book will change your life. And since your kitchen is such a huge part of your life, the change will be *big*.

And while you can totally skip around to what seems most helpful, following the book from start to finish will serve you best. Stick with me, and I promise on my collection of James McAvoy GIFs that this order will not fail you.

Ready to jump in and become obsessed with how awesome your kitchen is and how amazing you are inside it?

Let's go.

PART 1

Your Lazy Genius Kitchen

If you try to count the number of meals you will likely make over the course of your lifetime, you might weep. Since weeping would decidedly kill the fun vibe we're going for here, let's hurry along.

The point? No day escapes a food-related task, most days hold more tasks than you can count, and being in your kitchen feels like running on a turbo-charged hamster wheel that leaves you gasping for breath.

Allow me to hold your metaphorical face in my metaphorical hands as I say this: *of course* you're exhausted. Of course you are. Life in the kitchen doesn't provide any breathers to figure out what you're doing or what you need. Meals just keep coming no matter how much you need them to slow down.

Plus, you likely have never been taught the scope of skills to make your kitchen experience a little easier, but you feel stupid asking someone now because you're a grown person who pays utility bills, schedules dentist appointments, and buys retinol, so you're obviously supposed to know this stuff already.

First of all, it's fine that you don't know everything (spoiler: no one does), and second of all, I'm here to help.

The five steps I'm about to teach you will change your life in the kitchen literally forever. They are foundational to finding pain points, naming helpful solutions, and creating a sustainable rhythm in your kitchen for as long as you have one.

Remember that this part of the book is only about learning. You don't have to figure anything out yet. Maybe think of me as a fun, hip professor who's giving a fun, hip lecture (humor me here), and your only task is to absorb the information. No labs or practicums yet; that's Part 2.

Ready?

The first thing you need to do is *name what matters*. Always. It's foundational. Nothing else works until you name what matters, so that's our first step in creating a Lazy Genius kitchen.

prioritize

Name what matters most

What's the whole point of life in your kitchen? If you break it down to its essence, what's the purpose? What's the point? It's pretty simple, really:

You should have what you need, use what you have, and enjoy it.

Think about it. If you have everything you need *and* you use it, you'll enjoy your kitchen. It's what's extra, what's missing, and what lies unused that make your kitchen feel accidental.

Accidental or Idealistic?

A lot of people have *accidental* kitchens. For example, maybe your mom unpacked the boxes when you moved into your home, and everything is still where she put it three years ago. Even how you shop, plan, and gather around the table could be accidental. Sometimes you just *do stuff*. There's no real reason or purpose; it's just what you've always done.

Or maybe your kitchen and how you live in it are *idealistic*. You think it has to look a certain way, function within a specific system, and make you look and feel like you have your act together at every meal.

Neither Lazy nor Genius, accidental nor idealistic will serve you in the long term. Why? Because you don't know what matters most.

Even if you started over and built a kitchen from scratch, I'd bet my Benedict Cumberbatch poster that you'd be back where you are now in a matter of weeks—frustrated, overwhelmed, and picking up the phone for another night of takeout pizza.

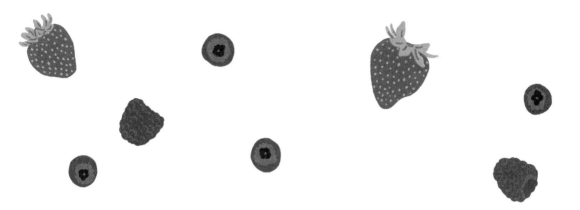

Without knowing *what matters to you*, even a new sparkly kitchen becomes accidental.

I know what you want. You want a kitchen that feels intentional but without making you try too hard for it. I have good news: that happens when you *prioritize* and name what matters most.

Why What Matters Matters

When you haven't figured out *what* matters, you implicitly allow *everything* to matter. You buy more stuff, sign up for more services, and reorganize more cabinets to try to make life easier. You spin off in a dozen directions, trying to make everything matter.

But it can't. It *just can't*. That's why your kitchen is cluttered and your brain is overwhelmed.

Unless you know what matters most about your space, your meals, how you plan them, and so forth, you'll simply tend to the most urgent need and repeat ad nauseam.

No one needs ad nauseam in the kitchen.

You need to prioritize.

When you prioritize what matters most, you see a clearer path to *your* best choices. You know clearly what to cook, organize, and renovate. You know what to buy, skip, and prep. You know if that chicken recipe is worth spending time on or not.

When you prioritize, you have a lens for choosing only what *you* need. And I promise it works.

How Do You Know What Matters?

You might be thinking, *This all sounds good, Kendra, but I don't* know *what matters most to me.*

Don't worry. You're not expected to know right away. Any time you need clarity on what matters, ask yourself these three simple questions:

1. What could matter?
2. What does matter?
3. What matters most?

It's basically a process of elimination. Not rocket science, I know, but it's a lot easier and exceedingly cheaper than a degree from MIT. Plus, it works. Before you start answering, though (that'll come in Part 2), let's break down how these questions get you to what matters.

What Could Matter

As an example, let's think about what *could* matter when you shop for food: price, quality, convenience, selection, experience, sustainability, and if a place has grocery pickup or shopping carts shaped like race-cars for your toddler. Those could all be important, right?

However, there is no grocery store on earth that can prioritize all those things. None. Whole Foods prioritizes quality and sustainability over price. Aldi prioritizes price over selection and experience. Trader Joe's prioritizes its personal identity over carrying multiple brands. Every store has to prioritize something, or it won't survive.

The same is true for you. *You have to prioritize.* If you try to tend to everything, you'll tend to nothing—at least not well. You have to drill down to what matters most *to you*, and the first step is listing all the possibilities.

Now, will all those possibilities likely be good, desirable qualities? Most definitely. Can they all matter? You want to say yes, so allow me to rephrase. Can they all matter *with equal value*? That's a big no.

But here's the good news: when you name what matters *most*, everything else falls into line without your having to give up as much as you think. When your priority is clear, it makes any sacrifices easier to swallow because you're getting what's most important.

There are "what could matter" lists for all six areas of your kitchen—space, meals, plan, food, prep, and table—coming up in Part 2, so don't worry about starting from scratch. (Kind Big Sister Energy coming through for you, pal.)

What Does Matter

Once you have your list of what could matter, you just start crossing stuff off. Now, for some people, that will prove a touch more difficult than for others. Choosing is just *the worst*. If you need some help narrowing down, here are two thoughts that could ease the process.

First, **live in the season.**

This is Lazy Genius Principle #4 (LGP #4), and it's one that offers the best permission to do what you need *right now*.

Your life in the kitchen is massively impacted by how much time, emotional margin, money, and many children you have. And those things change with each season of life.

As you narrow down the list of what *could* matter to what *does* matter, think about what matters *right now*. No ideals, no futures, no "when this changes." Right. Now.

When you live in your season, you know life will eventually be different while still embracing where you are now.

Second, **what makes you crazy?**

Identifying pain points is where the magic happens.

If you can name what makes you frustrated about cooking, your space, and even certain tools, you can more easily name what matters and therefore have a much better experience. No more yelling at inanimate objects! Huzzah!

Some examples of what could make you crazy:

- a nonstick skillet that everything gets stuck to
- a countertop covered with other people's junk
- having grocery lists in multiple places so you're always forgetting something
- kids that throw food on the floor
- having to go to five different stores to get the best deal
- splattering soup on your new Madewell sweater because you don't have a ladle and awkwardly use a coffee cup to serve it instead

When you name what makes you crazy, you have a clearer picture of your priorities.

So, when we get to those "what could matter" lists in Part 2, you're going to narrow them down to about three things each. If you have trouble, think about your season of life and what makes you crazy so you can gain some extra clarity.

And remember, only *you* can decide what matters most to you. It's okay if your short list looks different from everyone else's. You're allowed to care about what *you care about*.

What Matters Most

Now comes the hard part. You have to narrow your list of three down to one.

Before you start yelling at me, listen up. You're not dismissing what *does* matter outright. Your top three priorities will all play a role in how you experience your kitchen, but you need a *main thing*. Why? You want an engine that pulls the train. You want a sun that holds everything in orbit. You want a killer pair of jeans that are the foundation for all your amazing outfits.

What matters *most*? Naming this in all six areas of your kitchen will make you a Lazy Genius.

Real-life examples always help, so I'll share what matters most in my kitchen so you can see how this all plays out.

What Matters Most to Me

My current season of life involves writing this book during a pandemic, over the holidays, and within a tight timeline. Super chill. I also have three tremendously picky children. One doesn't like cheese or eggs. One doesn't like meat except salami. One doesn't eat sandwiches except on Thursdays. *It's a situation.*

If I were to ignore this season and keep chugging along like it's just me and my husband and all the time in the world, I'd be in a ball in the corner right now. Thankfully, I've Lazy Geniused my kitchen and picked what matters most. I'm upright and not in a corner!

Here's what this looks like . . .

What Matters to Me About Tools

Of all the qualities that could matter about my kitchen tools, I narrowed the list down to these three: **they work, they're well made,** and **they can go in the dishwasher**. If a tool fits all three of those qualities, I am supremely happy.

But sometimes those priorities conflict with each other. In that case, I need to know what matters *most*.

For me, it's functionality. I don't have a lot of time, my friend. I need my stuff to *work*.

I once went to an Airbnb that had only flimsy plastic cutting boards in the kitchen. When I tried to cut on them, they'd slide, it felt like the knife was hitting the counter beneath, and I started to feel crazy. No joke . . . I stopped cooking, went to Walmart, and bought a big wooden cutting board. I happily used it during my stay and left it as a gift for future vacationers.

That's how much function matters to me. I become slightly unhinged in a stranger's home and spend money on something I'll use for only three days. *Because that's what matters most to me.*

Back to my own kitchen. I already said that in addition to function, I want tools that are well made and can go in the dishwasher. However, high-quality tools are often divas and need to be washed by hand.

Listen, I *hate* washing dishes. It hurts my back, it makes my hands dry, and I'm legitimately grossed out when I have to reach into the lukewarm forgotten dishwater to let it drain. I do everything I can to avoid the process.

If I'm forced to choose between function or something being dishwasher-safe—for example, with a good knife—I choose function. I choose the knife. I choose to wash it by hand and cry a single tear and then move on with my life.

However, if a tool's function isn't sacrificed much when it goes in the dishwasher, I pick the tool that can go in the dishwasher. For example, wooden spoons are a general dishwasher no-no. The wood eventually cracks, and if that wood is reclaimed and hand-carved and an heirloom, the dishwasher will not be its friend. But if it's a cheap wooden spoon from a yard sale, I'll put it in the dishwasher with great enthusiasm until it cracks and I get another one. No harm done. Why?

Because I know what matters to me.

When you prioritize what matters, decisions are so much easier to make.

Here's another example.

What Matters to Me About Meals
My top three priorities from the *what could matter* list (that exists on page 70) are **brainless**, **tasty**, and **crowd-pleasing**, and that's been my top three ever since I started having kids over a decade ago.

During that time, I've slowly collected meals that fit all three priorities, and we eat them on a *very* frequent rotation. However, when one priority must take charge, what matters most to me is a meal that's **brainless**.

I love to cook, and I'm good at it. I love trying new flavors and learning new skills, but being a working mom means now is not my season to embrace that love. The time will come, and I'll love it when it does. For the time being, I want to cook meals I don't have to think about. I don't want to constantly fact-check instructions. I skip recipes that go against my cooking intuition. If a meal involves specific timing or deep attention, it's a pass.

That's why hot dogs and Tater Tots stay in our rotation right alongside chicken tikka masala. My brain doesn't work hard for either. Are hot dogs tasty to me? Not really. Do all three of my kids devour tikka masala? The little one is still on the fence.

But both meals are brainless. That means they get to stick around.

What Matters to Me About Shopping

Right now, I'm in the season of life where **convenience** is top, *top* priority. When my kids were babies and I had very little to fill my days, I used to shop at multiple stores to get the best price and the absolute best version of whatever ingredient I needed. Now, I barely have enough time for one store, let alone five or six, so I use Walmart grocery pickup almost exclusively. I order online and wait for a kind soul to load the food into my car. It's exactly what matters right now.

Do I sacrifice quality? Yes. Do I miss the experience at Whole Foods or Trader Joe's? Yes. Do I miss the savings I'd get from buying a few select things at Costco? Absolutely. But none of those are as important as the **convenience** of a Walmart a mile from my house that I don't even have to walk into to get what I need.

It will not always be that way, but I will embrace that it's that way right now. That's one of the best things about being a Lazy Genius. You live in your season (LGP #4) while it's here, know that life will eventually be different, and enjoy where you are as best as you can.

Prioritize Your Priority

Prioritize is step one because it is the only place to start. You *must* start with what matters. Everything in this book—I'm talking *everything*—hinges on your priorities.

But don't let that scare you. You can name what you think matters most, live with it, and if you realize that something else matters more, you can pivot. The world is not ending if you change your mind. In fact, expect to change your mind. It happens all the time because life is not white noise. It's dynamic and full of change. You have kids or then they move out, or you don't have them at all. You get a new job or quit the one you have. You move homes, cities, and states. You learn a new skill, buy a new pot, or get a new Trader Joe's down the street.

Life changes, and every time it does, your priorities likely will, too. Please be kind to yourself (LGP #13) as they do.

To recap, list what *could* matter, drill down to what *does* matter, and then do the hard but helpful work of naming what matters *most*. Your best decisions come from knowing what matters *most to you*. Name that one thing, and your kitchen will serve you well.

You will get a lot of prioritization reps throughout this book, and every time you go through the process, your confidence will grow. You're going to be an expert by the time we're done.

What could matter?
What does matter?
What matters **most**?

Once you know that, it's time for step two: essentialize. Let me teach you how to get rid of what's in the way.

essentialize

Get rid of what's in the way

Now that you've named what matters most, you know what *doesn't* matter anymore. It's time to see your space with new eyes and get rid of what's in the way.

I will forever be indebted to Greg McKeown for writing an entire book on this concept titled *Essentialism*. It was written primarily about vocation and career, but as it helped me rethink my work, I saw how getting rid of what's in the way impacts every area of life, including life in the kitchen. Maybe *especially* the kitchen. Accumulation and clutter have certainly shone bright in my kitchens over the years, and I'm guessing the same is true for you. Let's see what we can do about that.

Thankfully, essentializing like a Lazy Genius is inherently simple. **It's only about removal.** Nothing else.

So often, we organize first, but you can't organize until you essentialize. Otherwise, you're finding a home for things that don't need to be there. How many times have you bought some kind of storage solution for a thing you don't even use? You don't have to answer that. This is a judgment-free zone. But we all do it *because we go out of order* (LGP #11).

You must get rid of what's in the way **before** you put everything in its place (LGP #7).

The Noise of the Extra

When you fill your life with things that are not essential to what matters to you, you unintentionally add *noise* to your life. That can be the visual noise of cookbooks you don't open or the mental noise of unrealistic expectations. And managing noise, especially in the kitchen, is part of why you're always tired.

The irony is that our typical reaction to the noise is to *add more to it*.

You might think, for example, that your frustration is because your pots and pans are cheap and don't work well. While that might be true, if you buy a new set of pots without getting rid of the old ones, now you have double pots.

And what if the truer problem isn't the pots but, rather, that you were never taught a few basic cooking skills? New pots won't help that, but you buy them anyway, create more noise, and stay frustrated.

Adding to the noise is never the answer. **Essentializing** is.

Name what matters, and then get rid of what's in its way.

How to Know If Something Is Essential

Part 2 will walk you through multiple ways to essentialize your entire kitchen, but for now as you simply learn, start with this premise: **you have to choose whether or not something is essential.**

A lot of organization books like to claim there are rules about what and what not to keep, but I don't think that's true.

It's not fair for me to make a rule about *your* use.

Here's what I mean. Let's pretend there's a rule that says, "If you haven't used it in a year, you don't need it anymore." Sounds reasonable enough, right? But what if the item you're considering is your grandmother's mixing bowl that's too heavy to pull out quickly, too big to stay out on your current countertop, and too precious to casually use with little kids around? That bowl probably matters deeply to you, and just because you're not using it right now doesn't mean you should get rid of it—especially if you're pretty sure you will use it in another season of life. Maybe you do want to get rid of it, but that's not for me and my arbitrary rule to decide.

Only you can decide if something is worth keeping.
And you know what's worth keeping only if you name what matters.

Prioritize, then essentialize.

If you're stuck deciding whether or not to keep something, try this Decision Map. Not everything will follow it to the letter, but a lot probably will. If anything, it's a framework to help you narrow down why something is or isn't easy to let go of. Use it if you need it.

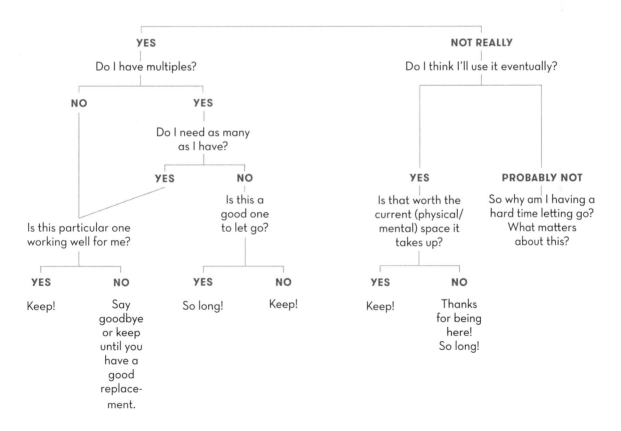

Do I Use This?

YES
Do I have multiples?

- **NO**
  Is this particular one working well for me?
  - **YES** Keep!
  - **NO** Say goodbye or keep until you have a good replacement.

- **YES**
  Do I need as many as I have?
  - **YES** Is this particular one working well for me? (connects to NO branch)
  - **NO**
    Is this a good one to let go?
    - **YES** So long!
    - **NO** Keep!

NOT REALLY
Do I think I'll use it eventually?

- **YES**
  Is that worth the current (physical/mental) space it takes up?
  - **YES** Keep!
  - **NO** Thanks for being here! So long!

- **PROBABLY NOT**
  So why am I having a hard time letting go? What matters about this?

While this works best for tangible items you can hold in your hand, it might work for mental stuff, too. Give it a go when you feel stuck on your essentializing journey.

What to Do with the Essentialized Stuff

This is the big question, right? Once you rip off the Band-Aid and are finally willing to say goodbye, you're left with the decision of where your stuff will go.

And that kind of decision often results in piles.

Oh, the piles.

The Lazy Genius way to deal with your piles is to limit their number and decide in advance (LGP #1) where they're going. Here's why.

When you're essentializing your physical kitchen, the temptation is to make All the Piles. One pile is for your sister, another is for a friend, a third is to sell online, a fourth is for a yard sale you might have, and yet another is to donate to the thrift store. This will come as no surprise: often when you make too many piles, they stay piles. You live in, around, and maybe under them. Congratulations, piles are your life now.

I understand wanting to pass things on to people who would really love them. High fives to you in that endeavor. But that endeavor will be far more successful if you *decide once* (LGP #1) how and when you'll share your stuff with your people.

Before you start opening cabinets, ask that friend if she wants any kitchen items you're getting rid of. She might not, and now you've eliminated an unnecessary pile.

Be honest about that imaginary yard sale. Consider if the thrift store actually wants your lidless Tupperware. Your desire to avoid waste is honorable, but sometimes it leaves you living in Pile World. Zero stars. Would not visit again.

If it works for you, my suggestion is to pick one exit path for everything you essentialize. Give everything the same path out—that is, batch it (LGP #9). It's enormously easier that way.

If you *need* multiple piles in order to recoup some much-needed cash or if your little sister is moving into her first college apartment and will indiscriminately take anything, think *now* about how you can keep those piles out of the way until they're on their way to their next home.

Finally, if you're worried you'll regret letting something go, put the essentialized stuff in a box in a closet or garage. Hold on to it but keep it out of sight. It'll likely become out of mind, which will often illuminate if you needed it in the first place. Maybe even set a calendar reminder for one, three, or six months from now to say a final goodbye if you haven't gone back for something.

Mental Piles

Piles are usually physical, but I've had mental piles, too.

When I let go of off-base expectations of how I should feed my family every day, those thoughts don't just disappear. Sometimes I'm left with a mental pile of words that have been my companion for so long that I don't know how to get rid of them. What do you do with *those*?

You do you, but it helps me to write them down.

I write out all the phrases and expectations that have been getting in the way of what matters so that I can see them, not just hear them in my head. It's almost as if the act of writing *physically removes them*, at least in part.

The way to remove them entirely is to replace them with new words. New expectations. New priorities. New permission.

If you've been telling yourself that you're not a good mom because your kids won't eat green vegetables, that's mental noise that does not support what matters—that is, being kind to yourself (LGP #13). Replace that noise with a better sound. Start small (LGP #2) by simply saying "My kids are happy I'm their mom, and it's okay if this process of getting them to eat food from the ground moves slowly." You don't have to read three self-help books, register for an online course from a child nutritionist, or buy tiny cookie cutters so you can make cucumber stars. Start small with the truth and see what happens.

Get rid of those mental piles, one by one.

The Rhythm of Essentializing

Again, we will go through the specifics of what and how you can essentialize the six areas of your kitchen, and I can't wait for you to experience those in your real life.

As we wrap up this part, though, I want to remind you that this isn't a one-time thing. Essentializing (LGP #10) is something to keep in mind whenever you feel frustrated by your space, your meals, how you plan them, what you shop for, the flow of your kitchen, and how you gather.

Always prioritize first; name what matters. Maybe what matters has changed, and your frustration will ease simply by naming that.

Or maybe your priority is the same, but there's something in its way. Keep an eye out for anything that's in the way. Practice this as often as you need to, one thing at a time. It won't be long before the craziness you feel turns to joy.

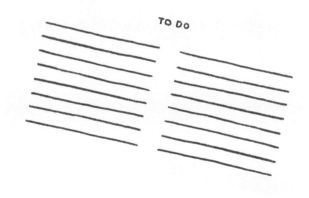

organize

Put everything in its place

You've named what matters. You've gotten rid of what's in the way. Next up?

You look at what's left and put it in its place. *Now* you organize.

I'm guessing you have a lot of expectations of how this should go. Organization is, after all, a massive industry. There is literally a store just for containers. And let's be honest . . . I love it, too!

But before you empty the trunk of your car to prepare for your shopping spree in the Home Organization section of Target, let's set some ground rules.

The Real Definition of Organization

Organization doesn't have to mean everything stacks, swivels, or has a label. It *can*, but it doesn't have to. It also doesn't mean you need to purge *everything* and become a minimalist. Again, you *can*, but it's unlikely the answer.

Organization is simply putting what matters in its place.

That's it. It can be pretty or ugly, functional or haphazard, rational or completely bizarre. All that matters is that you're serving what matters to *you*.

For example, in my family's kitchen, all our "crunchy things"—chips, pretzels, and anything else that comes in a bag—are "organized" by simply existing on the same pantry shelf. There are no stacks or bins or bags lined up in a row. They're just . . . there.

Now, is it like an arcade ball pit in there? Well, yeah, but *I don't care* because when it comes to organizing my food (which you'll do in Part 2),

I prioritize accessibility, not beauty or function. I can easily pull out the bag of barbecue chips even if it's covered up with bags of pretzels and Cheetos, and everything just settles into the empty space, kind of like pulling a ball out of a ball pit. That level of accessibility works for me, and I can let the rest go.

You can, too. Focus on what matters to you and organize in a way that supports it. You don't have to color-code your cookbooks or line up your cereals like little soldiers or make everything pretty enough for Instagram, if that doesn't matter to you.

The point? Put everything that matters in its place.

Reframe the Limits of Your Space

You can organize anything—thoughts, decisions, plans—but when you organize your *stuff*, you get an automatic failsafe.

Your space is finite.

You cannot pull a Molly Weasley and magically make your house bigger. The world of Harry Potter can teach us many things, but space expansion probably shouldn't be one of them.

Because your home—the pantry, your cabinets, that hall closet that holds the extra cereal—is finite, you do not have to choose your limits. They're already there in the form of shelves and drywall.

Embrace the limits of your space. Reframe how you feel about them.

Remember, Lazy Geniuses live in the season (LGP #4), and this might not be a season for stocking up when there's a sale, because you simply do not have the room.

I'm not trying to be a defeatist here; it's actually a good thing. Those limits help you clearly name what matters. If there's not a place for everything, you have to choose what's important enough to keep. Once you do, life feels simpler, not because you have less stuff but because you only have what matters most.

Ready to put everything in its place? Let's run through some tools that can help.

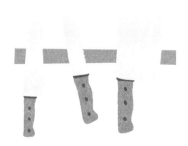

The Trifecta of Kitchen Organization

When you are considering how to group items—where they should go and where they should go in *relation* to each other—the Trifecta is a delight to use.

The Trifecta of Kitchen Organization is **type**, **task**, and **zone**.

They might feel eerily similar, but the differences matter. They're like a Russian nesting doll of organizational prowess, so let's break them down here so you can use them once we get to Part 2.

Organize by **type** based on *what something is.*
Organize by **task** based on *what something does.*
Organize by **zone** based on *where something happens.*

For example, you might store all your handheld tools together, like wooden spoons, tongs, and spatulas. That's organizing by *type*.

You likely use many of those handheld tools when you cook on the stove, so you might organize them near pots and pans that are also used to cook on the stove. That's organizing by *task*.

Finally, you might try to organize those handheld tools, pots, and pans near the place they are used—by the stove. That's organizing by *zone*.

Make sense? Type, task, zone.

Certain areas of your kitchen prefer one category over another, and sometimes they all work well together. In Part 2, I'll point out which of the Trifecta you can use when organizing something new.

A Quick Word on Making It Pretty

The chances are good that you want a pretty kitchen.

You want to open cabinets and be met with order. You want your counters, your recipe storage, your pantry, your table, the containers inside your fridge to be aesthetically pleasing. That's a real desire, and I stand in solidarity with it.

However, the tendency is to make something pretty before making it work. You think you won't mind the effort of getting a stepstool to reach the pretty bowl on the pretty open shelving that's just out of your reach every time you want cereal, but I'm pretty sure when you're tired and cranky and the rest of the kitchen is a wreck, *you will mind*.

Aesthetics could absolutely be your top priority, but please make sure a space is functional, too, especially before you spend the effort and cash on something that might not matter as much as you think it does.

Keep It Simple

Remember, you only organize what matters and then simply give it a home within the limits of your space, considering the Trifecta of type, task, and zone when it helps.

Put your stuff in its place day after day until your priorities change or until something is no longer essential.

Now that everything has a home in your kitchen, it's time for you to feel at home there, too.

personalize

Feel like yourself

Time for a little straight talk.

One of the reasons you don't like being in the kitchen is that you're trying to be someone else.

You think you have to be good at cooking and planning and gathering, but you're looking through a cripplingly specific lens. And when you hold yourself to these impossible standards of how you *should* be, you keep trying until you get it right or until you give up. That Lazy-to-Genius spectrum does not mess around.

Instead of trying to fit into someone else's mold, allow me to invite you to simply be yourself.

The Seven P's of Personalizing

To help you be yourself, I made up this thing called The Seven P's (**personality, people, priorities, proficiency, process, pleasure, and peace**) because if I don't use alliteration, my English degree will burst into flames. I'll give you an overview here, and in Part 2, we'll use The Seven P's to personalize specific aspects of your kitchen.

You have preferences like every human person, but you probably get stuck on occasion trying to figure them out. If you're a parent, it's especially tough to even remember what your favorite color is when all you do is wipe butts and ration Goldfish crackers.

Also (soapbox time) there is not a lot of cultural permission for women to name their preferences and then get to easily do them. A mom tries to take some time for herself, and suddenly guilt is everywhere trying to gain purchase on *the walls of her SOUL*. (That's the written version of my voice going up an octave.)

I promise this isn't going to be some deep philosophical chapter. You are reading a kitchen book, after all. But I also want you to feel the freedom to name what makes you feel like yourself so you can experience it in your kitchen.

Let's check out The Seven P's. (Are you imagining them as the Seven Dwarfs? Same.)

Personality

This is the most obvious one, right? You feel like yourself when you embrace your personality and act the way you most naturally want to.

For example, you might be a naturally reserved, observant, introverted person. You're not the one who carries a group conversation, but you're definitely invested in it when it happens. Still, you love quiet and not having to talk. That aspect of your personality probably feels natural when you're preparing dinner alone, but not so much when you have people over for a birthday dinner.

The tendency is to adjust who we are to fit the situation or the people we're around. If you're the host, you can't be quiet, right?

Or can you? (You can.) You can welcome your friends, say hello, ask them how they are, but you don't have to "turn up" the social part of your personality because "that's what hosts do." Your friends know you and love you for who you are; you don't need to adjust that person to fit a perceived expectation.

For me, I'm loud and talk fast and can be kind of intense. I mean, I'm not a parakeet. I generally know when I'm being annoying. But sometimes I get insecure being my full self when I'm around other people. If I have friends over, I might try to tone down my excitement or hold back the shriek I want to let out when they walk in the door, because that might be too much. But then guess what happens?

I don't feel like myself anymore.

The same probably happens to you.

If you're not yourself in your own kitchen, you're going to continue to struggle feeling at home there. Your enjoyment is cut off at the knees.

Pay attention to your personality when you're cooking ordinary dinners, when you're deciding meals for next week, and when you're setting extra places at your table for friends to join.

In all those circumstances, be who you are in your kitchen.

People

Who are your people? Who lives with you in your house? Who doesn't live with you but still feels at home?

People play a huge role in personalizing your experience in the kitchen, not only in how you act but in how you consider what *they* need, too.

It's one thing to adjust your personality because you think who you naturally are is somehow wrong. It's a different thing entirely to make adjustments to your plans and processes for the sake of someone you love. The first motivation is protection, while the second is *connection*.

This is why I don't redo housework that my husband, Kaz, does. Not that I need to, for the record. He's a grown man and can load a dishwasher as well as the next guy. However (and he would agree with this), we have different ideas of what a clean kitchen looks like. His definition is, well, messier than mine.

If he works hard to love me well by cleaning up after dinner, knowing full well how much I value a clean space, and then I go behind him and "fix it," that's putting my preference over my person. That's dismissing him for the sake of the toaster's being put back in the cabinet.

Name what matters most, especially when it comes to your people. To personalize something doesn't mean to have it your way; it's about feeling like yourself and allowing your people to feel the same way.

Priorities

You've already learned this part: name what matters. When you know your priorities, you can personalize how you do anything in the kitchen with greater intention.

If what matters most to you about cleaning the kitchen is to do it together as a family, then of course you want to do it as a family. But what if an aspect of your personality is to do things quickly? Sadly, children and efficiency are not always great partners.

So, what do you do? How can you feel like yourself? Is it by cleaning the kitchen quickly or cleaning the kitchen together? What matters most?

I won't answer that for you, but most potential frustrations are immediately neutralized when you remember what matters most. You relax and have the freedom to *feel like yourself*.

Proficiency

You could struggle feeling like yourself in the kitchen because you're trying to turn out meals like Martha Stewart, even though you're still not sure how to make a solid grilled cheese.

I'm not shaming you. A good grilled cheese takes practice (more butter than you think, and don't press down on the bread), but it's super unfair of you to beat yourself up for not being a better cook, a detailed planner, an organized shopper, or someone who can use a chef's knife without holding her breath.

Listen to me, dear one. *Listen.*

Being proficient at cooking, planning, prepping, and all those kitchen things does not always come naturally. It must be learned, which means someone must *teach* you. It often takes practice . . . lots of practice. But it starts with being *shown how.*

If no one teaches you to use tongs to toss spaghetti, you'll keep using your two spatulas and splattering your sweater with sauce and trying not to cry about it.

It's okay that you don't know stuff. It's okay if your proficiency isn't what you think it should be. Be kind to yourself (LGP #13), maybe even in extra doses as you learn what you don't yet know.

You will never feel like yourself in the kitchen if you're not kind to yourself for simply being there.

Process

Process will come into play when we start talking about how you'll systemize your Lazy Genius kitchen (that's the next step!), but it's important that how you naturally move through life—*how you process the process*—stays on your radar.

I'm currently typing this book on a computer as one does, and part of me is so daggum sad I can't write it on paper. *I love paper.* I love how I process my ideas and plans so differently on paper than how I do it digitally. It's just how I am. Maybe I can't apply that preferred process to the task of book writing, but I can to making a grocery list.

If other people rave about a meal planning app or digital shopping lists that are *so easy,* I remember how much I love the analog process and how it matters to me, and I decide to let someone else enjoy the app while I keep my pad of paper.

You should feel like yourself during the process of planning, prepping, and all the rest. If your preferred process is slow and steady, be slow and steady. If you prefer to cook everything in bulk because you love the process of batching (LGP #9), cook everything in bulk!

Respect your process. Embrace what makes you feel like yourself as you hang out in your kitchen.

Pleasure

What do you like? What makes you happy? What feels fun? What helps you take a deep breath and settle into yourself as you live life in your kitchen?

I want to say this one will come easily, but I fear it'll be one of the hardest for you to name.

Back to my soapbox. *So many women tell me they simply do not know what they like.* It's wild. And very sad. So, if that's you, this is your permission to reclaim or even claim for the first time what you love! What brings you pleasure, and how can you incorporate it into your Lazy Genius kitchen?

We'll cover lots of ideas in Part 2, but your pleasure could be open windows while you cook, music while you have a meal, a favorite pen while you make your shopping list, a mountain of fresh produce from the farmers' market after you shop, a beautiful cookbook to flip through as you plan . . . the possibilities are endless and personal.

And that's the gift, isn't it? It's personal. It's okay if what brings you pleasure in the kitchen is super different from your best friend, your mom, or even Oprah.

You get to decide what you love.

Peace

If your enjoyment in the kitchen was mathematically analyzed, I think peace would claim a decent percentage.

The kitchen can feel annoying for a lot of reasons, one of which is being super stressed by All the Things. Depending on your season of life, peace might not be there at all.

But when it's there? Game-changer.

So, what brings you peace? Personalize your Lazy Genius kitchen by naming what brings you peace.

Don't assume the answer is quiet or solitude or having nothing to do. Personally, I feel peaceful when I'm feeding a big crowd. My soul is, like, *ahhhhh, here we are, this is nice.* I love it. I feel settled and calm on the inside even though my outsides are stirring and cutting and in "bust it" mode.

As you think about what brings you peace, don't be bound by someone else's definition. It's great if peace means solitude, and it's great if peace means you're surrounded by people.

Again, *you decide what matters to you.*

And that's how The Seven P's can help you personalize.

Start Small

Listen. I know you. You're, like, WHAT ARE ALL THE WAYS I CAN PERSONALIZE EVERYTHING RIGHT NOW? SOMEBODY GET ME A PEN.

Deep breath, pal.

Your enthusiasm is beautiful, and I applaud it. Just remember to start small (LGP #2). If you start building a personalization machine, you'll spend more time maintaining its system than feeling like yourself.

Go slow. One thing at a time. Your kitchen isn't going anywhere, so learn to feel like yourself one step at a time.

Now that you've named what matters, gotten rid of what doesn't, put everything else in its place, and named how you can feel like yourself in the kitchen, it's time to put it all together into a flow.

systemize

Stay in the flow

The happiest times in my kitchen are the ones when my kitchen and I are in sync. That might sound strange, but it's real, and it's probably true for you, too.

Spatial, functional flow is a real thing, and it impacts your enjoyment, your efficiency, *and* your mental health. It's like those scenes in movies where the happy woman is cooking a meal and the drawer opens before she even reaches for it.

Flow.

Since you want to enjoy a kitchen rhythm and flow that works for *you*, you shouldn't use formulas or rules that hem you in. Nope. You need *principles*, and lucky for you, I told you about them in the intro.

(*Psst* to the people who skip intros. The list of principles is on page 49.)

Certain principles are well suited for certain situations, so throughout Part 2 I'll share my best principal picks for whatever area of the kitchen we're talking about.

But before that happens, we need a little systemizing pep talk.

Systems Alone Can't Save You

I consider myself a bit of a systems wizard, and I'm here to tell you that they can't fix everything. Sometimes it feels like they can't fix *anything*, and the sooner you embrace that, the more effective your systems will be.

Systems themselves aren't bad. In fact, some of us thrive on systems, on routines that keep us from turning into The Hulk. Or maybe you see the value in systems keeping you from turning into The Hulk so *much*.

But here's the problem. Too often, you let the system blindly lead instead of listening to your soul. You ignore rhythms in exchange for rules.

This is dangerously close to Genius territory, and I promise you that your incessant effort to create and manage "the perfect system" will result in your falling asleep in your clothes with a half-eaten Oreo in your hand. (Actually, who are we kidding? There's no such thing as a half-eaten Oreo.)

If you're clinging to systems or even to the *idea* of the ones we're about to create, please remember their proper place. Sure, systems are amazing and even life-changing, but *only* when they support what matters to you and even more so when you show yourself kindness if they fall apart.

Finding the best way to do something isn't always best for your soul.

Labeling every bin and basket in your life doesn't give *you* a name and a purpose.

Giving everything a place doesn't define *your place* in the world.

If you're crying, I'm sorry. Dry your tears!

Logistics are coming! Logistics are coming!

Why You Systemize with Principles and Not Rules

Think of your systems less like a machine and more like a boat on a river. Remember, the point is to stay in the *flow*.

Sometimes you go fast, sometimes slow, sometimes you get turned around or hit rapids that are trying to murder you, sometimes you take a break to rest on the shore, and when it's time to keep going, the water is still moving and waiting for you to ease back in.

Because that's what life does, right? It keeps moving whether you want it to or not.

That is especially true of life in your kitchen.

If you don't pay attention to the flow, life will still keep moving, the water will get rougher, and you'll feel like you're holding on for dear life at every turn.

So, instead of letting the river get all jammed up or turn into a waterfall or whatever happens to rivers, use a Lazy Genius principle or two to stay in the flow. A few simple choices will make the trip more pleasant, even when those rapids come.

How to Choose the Best Principles for Your Situation

As we look specifically at the six areas of your Lazy Genius kitchen (space, meals, plan, food, prep, and table), only you will know what you need. My examples might land sometimes, but often you will do a better job of Lazy Geniusing your situation than I will, simply because I don't know your life.

Since you do, here's how *you* decide what principle works for you.

Is your situation out of *order*, out of *rhythm*, or out of *sorts*? The type of challenge helps you know the type of principle to choose.

When something is out of order, you need a quick win to get back to equilibrium.

When something is out of rhythm, you need a solution to consistently work on a regular basis.

When something is out of sorts, most likely you, you need a renewed perspective, something to keep you focused on what really matters.

OUT OF ORDER
principles are:

Decide Once,
Start Small,
Ask the Magic Question,
and
Put Everything In Its Place.

OUT OF RHYTHM
principles are:

Build the Right Routines,
Set House Rules,
Batch It,
Essentialize,
and
Go in the Right Order.

OUT OF SORTS
principles are:

Live in the Season,
Let People In,
Schedule Rest,
and
Be Kind to Yourself.

Categorizing the thirteen Lazy Genius principles in this way helps you limit your choices and find a solution and a deep breath a little faster.

Simply run your situation past the lens of each of the thirteen principles, and see which ideas resonate the most. Some will be eureka moments and others will be quieter. Choose whatever you like.

A Lazy Genius Kitchen Recap

You did it! You've learned the five steps you need to Lazy Genius any part of your kitchen. (And, by the way, lots of other places, too. I can tell you right now I am *not* writing *The Lazy Genius Bathroom*, so you can use the steps to figure out that one on your own.)

Here are the five steps one final time:

PRIORITIZE	ESSENTIALIZE	ORGANIZE	PERSONALIZE	SYSTEMIZE
Name what matters to you. You get to decide.	Get rid of what's in the way. Anything that doesn't support what matters is just noise, so turn down the volume.	Put everything in its place. The limits are permission to choose what matters most.	Feel like yourself in your kitchen by focusing on your preferences without apology or guilt.	Keep the flow going with any combination of Lazy Genius principles you want to use.

You got it? Ready to apply these to the six specific areas of your kitchen? I wish you could see my face right now, dear reader. My teeth could fall out, I'm smiling so big.

Let's keep Lazy Geniusing your kitchen!

Have What You Need

BUTTER

BUTTER

BUTTER

Now that you have the five steps you need to Lazy Genius your kitchen, it's time to put them into practice. Remember, the kitchen is too broad to approach all at once, so we'll start small (LGP #2) and go in the right order (LGP #11) with these six areas:

1. **SPACE:** We're starting here because it's the container for everything else.

2. **MEALS:** What you cook depends on how your space functions and the tools you keep within it. Plus, meals are kind of important since they happen always.

3. **PLAN:** How you decide what to cook depends on what meals you eat.

4. **FOOD:** What you shop for depends on what you planned.

5. **PREP:** Now that you have food for the meals you've planned in a space that works, you continually ready your space for the next thing.

6. **TABLE:** And then we gather.

You can certainly skip around, but if your kitchen could use a decent Lazy Genius overhaul, this is the order you want.

In each of the six sections, we'll apply the five steps, and you'll be doused in perspective and practical tools that will ensure you have what you need *for your kitchen.*

Let's jump in.

space

Your actual kitchen + all the stuff inside

You're in your kitchen all the time, so of course you'd like to enjoy being there.

Maybe you're *trying* to like it, but so far nothing has worked. It's possible you're stuck in either the Genius Way or the Lazy Way, but you haven't yet discovered the Lazy Genius Way. Here's what I mean. . .

Stuck in the Genius Way

It's easy to assume the Genius Way is desirable, but as we've already learned, being all Genius means spending excessive energy on things that don't matter to you. If this is your mindset, maybe you expect your kitchen to resemble a rom-com movie set or the "after" of an episode of *Fixer Upper*. If it's not ideal, it doesn't count.

A genius thinks the countertops must be quartz, the appliances must be top-notch, and the drawers must be soft-close. The pots must nestle snuggly, the plates must be ceramic with unfinished edges, and you need every tool that Real Simple, Martha Stewart, Chrissy Teigen, and your mom say is important. Open shelving is optional but pre-ferred, as long as you have tastefully mismatched glassware. There is little room for partial solutions or plastic.

While all that might look nice in a magazine, it's exhausting to accomplish in real life with real people. And that brings us to the oppo-site mindset, the Lazy Way, which is easier to accomplish but equally unfulfilling.

Stuck in the Lazy Way

Since you can't have your dream kitchen, you exist in a nightmare, using broken tools on cluttered counters because it's all or nothing, baby, and you've chosen nothing.

You resent your kitchen for not meeting your expectations; resent your kids for always requiring food; and resent your spouse, your boss, or yourself for not providing more money to make things better.

You're secretly embarrassed that you use a spatula to get spaghetti sauce out of a pan because no one ever told you the right tool to use, and you're thirty-seven and feel stupid asking someone about it now.

You lean into hot dogs and boxed mac and cheese, not so much because of your season of life but because you just don't care anymore or are too afraid to admit how much you *do*. You know there's got to be a better way, but you're too overwhelmed to find it.

Rejoice, reader! I bring you the Lazy Genius Way!

The Lazy Genius Way

Lazy Geniuses experience life in the kitchen with purpose *and* permission to chill out when necessary.

> They have what they need.
> They use what they have.
> They enjoy their space because it's built around what matters to them.
> They're fine if everything isn't perfect because priorities are named and tended to.
> They actually *like* being in the kitchen.

Are you ready to Lazy Genius your space? Of course you are.

Let's create a space that makes sense for you with our five Lazy Genius steps:

1. **prioritize:** name what matters

2. **essentialize:** get rid of what's in the way

3. **organize:** put everything in its place

4. **personalize:** feel like yourself

5. **systemize:** stay in the flow

Whenever you want to burn up your kitchen and start over, put down the matches and try these five steps first.

Let's go.

Step One Prioritize Your Space

The Objective: Name what matters most.

Lazy Geniuses go in the right order, so we start with *what matters to you.*

Remember, we narrow our choices by thinking about what *could* matter, moving to what *does* matter, and then making the seemingly impossible but legit amazing decision of what matters *most.*

Let's do that now with your space.

What *Could* Matter in Your Space?

Things that could matter include:

- **Access:** You can get to everything quickly and easily.
- **Storage:** All your stuff has a home.
- **Ease:** Your tools and surfaces are low maintenance.
- **Quality:** You want to invest in what will last a long time.
- **Versatility:** You want one tool for seven tasks.
- **Feel:** You like the vibe of your space.
- **Calm:** Nothing is crammed, piled, or cluttered.
- **Kid-Friendly:** Your tiny humans are comfortable in the kitchen and know how to find what they need.
- **Aesthetics:** You want the space and your tools to be pretty and reflect your style.
- **Functionality:** Everything does its job well.
- **Gathering:** There's room for all the people to sit and hang out, and you have plenty of glasses and serving bowls to feed them generously.

Certainly, we could name more, but those are likely some heavy hitters. Read through the list, pay attention to how you feel as you go, and now we'll narrow down.

What *Does* Matter in Your Space?

This might feel difficult because you're so used to prioritizing every-thing, but in Part 1, we already covered two ways to eliminate some options: **live in the season** and **pay attention to what makes you crazy**.

You're not trying to prioritize for the rest of eternity; just think about what makes sense for your season *right now*.

Once you name that, move to the crazy. Jot down a few things about your space and the tools within it that create a deep desire in you to throw something against the wall.

If after those two filters you're still struggling to reduce your "what does matter" list to three things, try these questions on for size.

What do you cook?

You need a space equipped to bring your meals together in the tasti-est, most helpful way possible, so naming what *kinds* of meals you tend to cook will ensure you have the tools and atmosphere you need.

What's in your rotation? Think salads, tacos, sheet-pan meals, noo-dle bowls, grain bowls, soup, stuff on the grill, pizza, pasta, etc. What do you need from your space and tools to support what you cook day after day?

Who do you feed?

How many meals come from your house every day? How often do you have people over?

If you have three kids who eat cereal for breakfast and cafeteria food for lunch, you can prioritize dinner rather than all three meals. If you host a big group from your church once a month for a meal *and that matters*, your space and tools should support feeding large crowds.

On the flip side, if you use an entire cabinet to store tools from that one time you hosted your family for Thanksgiving but likely won't do it again for another decade, maybe you'd be happier using your space another way.

Have you narrowed down to three? Don't move on until you do.

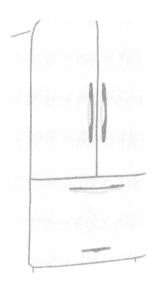

What Matters *Most* in Your Space?

You can do this.

Of your three priorities, choose the one that matters most. Remember that the limit is freeing, not restrictive. Knowing what matters most about your space makes you more content weirdly fast.

For example, you'll feel better buying that Dutch oven because it fits your priorities instead of feeling guilty for buying something at all. *Or* you'll know to skip the Dutch oven because you prioritize simplicity and don't need multiple giant pots, no matter how pretty they are.

Prioritize

Have What You Need

Now that you know what matters most about your space, you can better understand what you need from your kitchen and the tools inside it.

First, do you have everything you need? If you prioritize hands-off cooking because you work full-time, do you have a slow cooker?

If you prioritize an easy cooking experience, is your counter clear and ready for you to jump into dinner, or do you use it to store more things than are helpful?

Make sure you have what you need. Chances are, there might be something that matters that you don't have yet. Think through what that might be.

If you're a list person, you can be super linear and ask yourself "What choices, tools, or changes would make this priority happen every day without a hitch?" Write down your answer, and then take small steps toward getting those things in the coming days.

Or you can *experience* your kitchen for a week or so through your new lens of what matters most. Simply pay attention to what helps and what's in the way, adjusting as you go. Move that bowl of fruit. Switch the mugs to another cabinet. Keep an eye out for a sale on the Instant Pot.

As you live with what matters most, make sure you have what you need.

One of the areas where we get overwhelmed with what we need is *kitchen tools*. Let's talk about those next.

A New Way to See Your Tools

The internet is packed with lists of must-have kitchen tools for "every kitchen," but here's the thing: your must-haves won't always match everyone else's. Don't get distracted by other people's lists because they're just that—other people's lists.

Your must-have tools are the ones you use. Your priorities are your priorities, and life is better when you stick with the tools that support those priorities.

I already mentioned my hatred for washing dishes, so a high priority for me is avoiding said chore at all costs. Therefore, most of our meals need one cooking vessel, but it has to hold a meal big enough for my family of five. That means my must-have tools include a couple of really big sheet pans, a large Dutch oven, and a skillet that's bigger than a preschooler.

We rarely cook sides (again, dirty dishes), so I don't need a lot of saucepans. I have two—*just two!*—and they hold simple syrup more often than they do green beans. Other cooks might be appalled at my lack of cookware, but it serves what matters most to me.

Your list is your list. Own it.

As you consider your own must-haves, you might need some help knowing what tools do what tasks. Good news! There's an entire section in Part 3 (page 161) all about tools—what they do and how to use them, all so you can have what you need and skip the rest.

You don't need every tool for every skill. You just need what matters to you.

Use What You Have

If you don't know how to use a helpful tool, it's just in the way. (I'm looking at you, Instant Pot.)

When you don't know how to use something, you have two choices: *learn* or *let it go.*

If you do, in fact, own an Instant Pot you don't know how to use, I have good news: "How to Use Your Instant Pot" is on page 166, *but* the point here is that if you have what you need, it doesn't do you any good if you don't use it.

You have to *use* a tool for it to go in your Lazy Genius kitchen, so choose what tools, both big and small, make sense for you and then commit to learning them. That way they can do their job of serving what matters most *to you.*

As you look at your space and your tools, and notice things you thought you needed but don't actually use, maybe it's time to say goodbye because that thing is just in the way, right?

And that, my friend, is why we essentialize. Time for step two.

Step Two Essentialize Your Space

The Objective: Get rid of what's in the way.

This is probably the most hands-on part of the book, simply because it's *all the stuff in your whole kitchen*. A lot could be in the way in all those cabinets and drawers, so before you start emptying everything out and living in the Land of Piles again, let's make a plan.

First, **let people in** (LGP #8).

This means a few things. First, if you live with other humans and plan to Lazy Genius your space in the near future, let people know and let them help. Ask for help with the essentializing itself. Ask your family to figure out dinner tonight. Ask a neighbor if your kids can play at her house for an hour.

Second, let people in by asking that sister or best friend if she wants any of the stuff you don't need anymore. Remember that? You need to make a plan *now* (decide once, LGP #1) where most of your stuff will go so you can avoid the piles.

Second, **start small** (LGP #2).

You don't have to deal with your entire kitchen today. In fact, very much do not do that unless you have no humans or responsibilities that need tending *and* you slept really well last night. A kitchen clean-out all at once sounds fun in theory, but it's exhausting and rarely sees the end of the road before today's sun goes down.

Start small so you'll actually *do* something, and that small something will likely have a bigger impact than you think.

My favorite way to start small when I'm essentializing a space is with The First Pass.

The First Pass

The First Pass is like an essentializing blitz. Take five minutes and only remove the obvious things that are in the way. Now that you've prioritized, you'll know it when you see it. If you're unsure, leave it.

Possibilities could include mail on the counter, a coffee pot you've been meaning to get rid of, a pretty jar that holds tools you don't use, sippy cups your kids have outgrown, a pot with a broken handle . . . again, you'll know it when you see it.

Usually the culprit of an overwhelming kitchen is just extra stuff you don't need, not bad organization. Get rid of what's in the way and see what happens. Removing a few items will have a bigger impact than you think.

The Second Pass

When you have a little more time, do The Second Pass. This is where you get curious.

Do you have an entire shelf dedicated to wineglasses because you got them for a wedding present, but they are literally dusty on the shelf because you've never had sixteen people over for wine in your life? Maybe you've kept them because ideally you'd love to have a giant dinner party where everyone has their own wineglass, like a grown-up.

Look deep into my eyes and repeat after me: A Lazy Genius kitchen is not an ideal kitchen. It's a kitchen to serve and brighten your life *right now*. Right now might not be the season of life for sixteen glasses of wine, and that is okay.

Be curious about why your space holds what it holds and exists the way it exists, all through the lens of what matters most to you.

If you need help deciding what to keep and what to let go of, check out that Decision Map (page 33).

Remember, don't organize yet. Just assess and remove. Feel free to do it slowly and one small space at a time.

You're doing great.

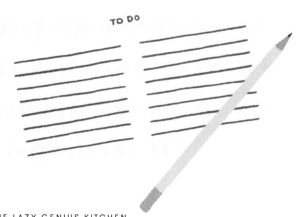

Step Three
Organize
Your Space

The Objective: Put everything in its place.

Your kitchen holds multiple items for multiple tasks happening multiple times a day. It has to provide for your early morning coffee, a 10:00 a.m. toddler snack, and your book club or teenager's soccer team coming for dinner. It's as if your kitchen is a quick-change artist charged with keeping your family alive. That's quite a job description.

The best way your space can serve you is if you have what you need and use what you have, both of which are highly impacted by *knowing where things are*. So, now that your space has been essentialized based on what matters most to you, it's time to organize what's left.

Remember, organization doesn't have to be "labeled order" unless that matters to you. It's just putting everything in its place (LGP #7).

How to Know If You Need to Organize Your Space

If you can find what you need when you need it, essentializing might have been enough! No organization needed. Just because we're talking about it, that doesn't mean you have to do it.

Look around your kitchen. Is your space functioning well for you? Can you find what you need? Are your priorities in line with how your kitchen is already organized? Great!

However, if you think a little organization is merited, let's talk about how to do it.

Organize by Zone

In Part 1, we talked about the Trifecta, organizing by type, task, or zone. Listen, when it comes to organizing your kitchen space as a whole, zones reign supreme.

Because you do such a variety of tasks in your kitchen and need all kinds of tools to do them, organizing your space by zones—that is, *where* something happens—will serve you well.

These are some examples of zones:

- **The Dinnerware Zone:** Plates, bowls, silverware, and napkins are together near where you eat or near the dishwasher.
- **The Drink Zone:** Cups, mugs, tumblers are all close to your coffeemaker or bar cart.
- **The Cooking Zone:** Pots, pans, and utensils are close to the stove.

- **The Prep Zone:** Storage containers, foil, and plastic wrap are close to the fridge.

You see that? Different items are grouped together based on *where they happen*. That's organizing by zone.

Chances are excellent you already implement zones. You just might not do it with intention, so let's add some.

Assess Your Current Zones

Take two minutes to see if your current storage zones make sense. You might not realize things aren't working because you haven't asked.

Look around and notice if your general organization serves what matters most to you. You've done most of the work already in getting rid of what doesn't belong anymore, and now you can put what's left in its best space.

Would anything benefit from a move? Are your bowls in one cabinet and your plates in another? Are you frustrated by how often your daughter asks for a drink because she can't reach the cups and maybe if you move them to a drawer or lower cabinet she could do it herself? Are your coffee mugs unusually far from the coffeemaker?

Just look around.

Pro tip: If you need a visual of where things *could* go, grab a sticky note pad, write down your zones, and move the stickies around instead of the stuff. It's much easier to try things out in your imagination.

When Starting from Scratch

Maybe you got overzealous, did *not* use your imagination, and pulled everything out already. Maybe you're moving into a new kitchen and want to think through your zones from the beginning. Or maybe you just find great comfort in clearing the decks.

Regardless, if you're starting from scratch, organization requires just two steps.

1. Big rocks first.
2. Fan out.

Big Rocks + Fan Out

Big rocks are things that have only one option, and that's why they go first. Remember, Lazy Geniuses go in the right order (LGP #11), so starting with items that have zero flexibility makes sense.

Think about items that have limited storage possibilities, like pots and pans. There are only so many places those can go. I have a giant stockpot I use maybe once a year, and it's so tall, there is literally only one cabinet in my kitchen where it will fit. Better for me to use that cabinet for that pot rather than for other stuff that could go somewhere else.

Big rocks don't have to be about size either; they could be about *priority*.

If beverages give you life and are a top priority in how you experience your kitchen, they deserve a dedicated zone, even at the expense of something else. It's better to save prime space for a prime purpose.

Start with what can go in just one place or is important enough to get first dibs.

Next, **fan out**. Pick the next most important thing and give it its best home. Keep going until there's nothing left. That's it.

By the way, don't forget that traditional storage containers aren't your only option. Just because a big jar says "utensils," that doesn't mean it's what you have to use to store utensils. I store my cooking utensils in a vintage planter. It's bigger, prettier, and most important, it gives me better access—a top priority for my tools.

Bowls can go into drawers. Glasses can go into lower cabinets. Dishtowels can live in a wire basket on your counter instead of in a drawer.

You decide what matters. Put things where they make sense for your space, not anyone else's space. Who cares if it's weird as long as it works.

Remember the point. Just put everything in its place.

Now that your stuff has a home, it's time for you to feel at home, too.

Step Four
Personalize Your Space

The Objective: Feel like yourself.

Isn't that really what this all comes down to? You just want to be a person in your kitchen and like it most of the time.

Time to remember The Seven P's: personality, people, priorities, proficiency, process, pleasure, and peace.

Run through the list and consider how you can feel like yourself *in your space* and *with your tools* based on any of these seven things.

For example, if you notice how music gives you **pleasure** or brings you **peace** while you get a meal together, play music. Maybe even be a genius about it, since *it matters*. Save up for a great Bluetooth speaker to keep in the kitchen, spring for a paid Spotify account where you can have more control over the song order, or move the old record player from the den into the kitchen where it'll be enjoyed even more.

If your **personality** needs visual **peace** in the form of minimal clutter, organize your kitchen so that as little as possible is on the counters. If you have open shelves that drive you crazy because of how messy the stacks look, store large items like beautiful pots or cookbooks on those shelves instead and move the mess behind closed doors.

If your **process** is to cook a lot at once, organize your space in such a way that a large stretch of counter space is always clear so you can set up camp without having to move a lot out of the way.

If bright colors bring you **pleasure**, store those colorful silicone spatulas in a striking urn, replace your white dishtowels with patterned ones, and prioritize a spot on the counter for your regular bundle of daisies from Trader Joe's.

Personalize your space. Personalize your tools. Make your kitchen your own, no one else's, because when you Lazy Genius your kitchen, your entire home feels better.

Now that everything is in its place and you feel like yourself, let's figure out how to live in your kitchen and maintain its Lazy Genius status day after day.

Step Five
Systemize
Your Space

The Objective: Stay in the flow.

Systemizing your space is simply making sure things go where they're supposed to.

You already have what you need, you're going to become more proficient in using the tools you have, and you're going to make organizational and stylistic choices that make you feel like yourself.

The point for your space is just to keep it that way, and we'll use Lazy Genius principles to do it.

Remember, you can use whatever principles you like, but I've handpicked a few that I think rise to this particular occasion quite well.

Principal
Picks for
Your Space

Put Everything in Its Place (LGP #7)

We already covered this in great detail . . . I mean, it's a whole step! But it is easily the most important principle for your space, so I'm saying it again.

Your system will find a pleasant rhythm when things are *where* you expect them to be *when* you expect them to be there. That means everything is in its place *and* everything is consistently *put back* in its place. If you get lazy and don't put things in their place, your system will deteriorate before it's even had a chance.

Please give your system a chance!

Which leads us to . . .

Build the Right Routines (LGP #5)

As a Lazy Genius, you don't create a routine by doing four tasks in a certain order. You create a routine by naming where you want to go. The routine is like an on-ramp to somewhere specific, not what you do step by step.

As you think about systemizing your space, name what you love about being in your kitchen and build your routine from there.

Is your cooking enjoyment higher when you start with a tidy space? Build a routine to have a clean kitchen before you start dinner.

Do you love cooking when you listen to a podcast, as opposed to those weird YouTube videos your kids watch? Build a routine to put in your earbuds and listen to a favorite show when you first enter the kitchen. (I hear *The Lazy Genius* podcast is, like, really great.)

Do you groan when you walk into the kitchen every morning and there are still remnants of dirty dinner dishes and evening snacks not put away? Build a routine to have the family clear the counters before everyone goes to bed.

Systemizing your space will benefit greatly from one or two Lazy Genius routines.

House Rules (LGP #6)

House Rules are what they sound like—rules that everyone in the house knows and mostly follows. I love House Rules because they're the gate-keepers that prevent things from becoming chaotic.

Create a House Rule that supports what matters to you.

Do cluttered countertops get in the way of your space function-ing at its best? Make a House Rule that no mail/bookbags/laundry is allowed on the counter.

Does it matter that your tools last? Make a House Rule that your good knives can never, ever, *ever* go in the dishwasher.

Does it matter that you can listen to a podcast (especially mine, *wink wink*) while you cook? Make a House Rule that no one is allowed to take your kitchen pair of earbuds. They are sacred. Leave them be.

Be Kind to Yourself (LGP #13)

There will be tools that get the best of you. There will be knives that slip, Instant Pots that don't lock, and garlic presses that don't press.

You're still doing great. No one comes out of the womb knowing how to use the entirety of a Williams-Sonoma catalog, so chill out on the criticism of your own skills. We're all constantly learning, and you are no exception.

When to Apply a Principle

Remember, the primary objective for systemizing your space is to enjoy a rhythm that works, not to place more rules on your life.

Pay attention to when that rhythm hits a speed bump. When does it lose its flow? That's a place to apply a principle and see if the flow returns. Don't overthink it. Just consider a principle when frustration hits.

Go slow, start small, and be patient.

Big systems don't hold up anyway, so steer clear.

Remember the Path for Your Space

First, *prioritize*. Name what matters most. When you know this, clarity will quickly follow.

Second, *essentialize*. Be on the lookout for items in your kitchen or ways you use your space that no longer serve you, and let them go.

Third, *organize*. Please, oh please, do not do this unless you know all your stuff actually matters.

Fourth, *personalize*. Make sure you feel like yourself in your kitchen, whether it's based on your personality, your process, or what brings you peace.

Finally, *systemize*. Once everything is in its place, enjoy the rhythm of your kitchen. Tend to it. Pay attention to how things are working. Put your stuff away. Use Lazy Genius principles to find a flow whereby your kitchen serves you and not the other way around.

Congratulations, you just Lazy Geniused your space.

Now it's time to do the same with the meals you cook.

meals

What you eat every day

Meals are a series of unending questions with crapshoot answers.

Is it time to eat?
What should I have?
What will he want?
Can I make this before she gets cranky?
Do we have that ingredient?
Is this worth another dirty pan?
Will she eat that?
Will this taste good?
Can I make this without ruining it?
Where did I put that recipe again?
Does cereal count as dinner?
Will my kids ever know how to cook for themselves?
HOW ARE THEY STILL HUNGRY?

The next meal is always around the corner, the cycle never stops, and your frustration absolutely checks out. I know you want to fix it, and these might be two ways you've tried. I'm guessing if they worked, you wouldn't be reading this book.

Stuck in the Genius Way

You aim for every single meal to be healthy, seasonal, fast, inexpensive, kid-friendly, comforting, and delicious. Every single one.

(This is generally impossible, by the way.)

You over-plan, over-buy, and get in over your head. Your shelf is stacked with cookbooks containing potentially magical recipes, but either you haven't found the magic yet or you don't have what it takes to make it work.

You aim too high and beat yourself up for not getting it right.

Stuck in the Lazy Way

You resent that not every meal can be healthy, seasonal, fast, inexpensive, kid-friendly, comforting, and delicious, so you give up.

You can't cook everything so you might as well cook nothing. You depend on bags and boxes of brown foods to get you through, and you roll your eyes at people who make kale for dinner, assuming they think they're better than you. (They're not; you're both great.) You know there's a better way, but you'd rather watch TV than figure it out.

I figured it out for you.

It's the Lazy Genius Way.

The Lazy Genius Way

As a Lazy Genius, you . . .

Know what meals fit your season of life.

Have deep appreciation for both hot dogs and homemade soup.

Know how to make simple food taste good.

Might be afraid of messing up a recipe, but that doesn't stop you from trying.

Enjoy making meals in your kitchen and are kind to yourself when you don't.

Doesn't that sound nice? I promise it's possible. It's time to take your meals through our five-step Lazy Genius process so that you can finally enjoy cooking them.

1. **Prioritize:** Name what matters most.

2. **Essentialize:** Get rid of what's in the way.

3. **Organize:** Put everything in its place.

4. **Personalize:** Feel like yourself.

5. **Systemize:** Stay in the flow.

Even if you feel on top of your meal game now, these five steps will always be here for you when you need a reset.

Here we go!

Step One
Prioritize
Your Meals

The Objective: Name what matters most

When it comes to the food you eat every day, so many things could matter. It might be the most overwhelming thing to prioritize. That doesn't mean you should stop reading (you can do this!), but I get the overwhelm of trying to make every meal for every purpose.

The sooner you release the expectation of making everything matter, the sooner you'll enjoy what actually does.

What *Could* Matter About Your Meals?

Here's your list to get you thinking:

- **Easy:** Doesn't require a lot of skill
- **Simple:** Has limited steps and few ingredients
- **Brainless:** Can be made on autopilot, even if the recipe isn't easy or simple
- **Seasonal:** Uses fresh ingredients, ideally from a local farm or your own garden
- **Tasty:** The food itself has amazing flavor and makes you excited to take the next bite
- **Crowd-Pleasing:** Everyone eats it with minimal complaint
- **Healthy/Balanced:** Meets your personal requirements for nutrition
- **Versatile:** Can easily accommodate ingredient substitutions
- **Different:** Is not like the same meal over and over again
- **Inexpensive:** Doesn't kill the food budget
- **Fast:** Takes little time to get on the table
- **Comforting:** Nourishes your soul
- **On-the-Go:** Can be grabbable and portable
- **Ready When You Are:** Can be made in advance and reheated easily

For real. It's a lot. And all of them sound great, right? But as we've discussed, you can't prioritize them all, plus some are even in conflict a bit. You can't be in a battle over what matters, so it's vital that you choose. No mercy.

What *Does* Matter About Your Meals?

Your keys to narrowing this down are to **live in the season** (LGP #4) and **pay attention to what makes you crazy**, but I'm guessing your season is a major factor in naming what matters most.

Consider how your meals need to serve your life during the immediate future. I usually think about my family's priorities only for the next one to three months, simply because so much can change how our meals come to the table.

You might not always eat the way you wish you could, but embracing your season makes it easier to enjoy.

What Matters *Most* About Your Meals?

I know the process of naming one thing feels limiting, but limits always help you know where to go. When you know what you're looking for, it's easier to find it. This is especially true of meals.

If what matters most is convenience, you're probably not going to soak your own beans.

If what matters most is not having to think, you're probably not going to try a lot of new recipes.

If what matters most is trying exotic flavors, you're probably not going to find them in your Julia Child cookbook. (I mean, I love her. She just doesn't use a lot of cardamom.)

If a recipe or meal doesn't serve what matters most, leave it for another time and Google something else. It's that simple.

Three Squares a Day

Consider how what matters most to you impacts breakfast, lunch, and dinner. Often we focus on just dinner, but different meals have different vibes. It's good to flesh out your top priority across your entire day.

At our house, all our meals are brainless, even breakfast and lunch.

I make waffles, pancakes, pumpkin bread, and bacon in giant batches every few weeks and freeze them. Every morning, my kids can heat any of that in the microwave or grab something they can make themselves, like cereal or oatmeal. This mama is hands-off in the mornings.

For lunch, our kids get what we call a Field Trip Lunch. A sandwich, two fresh foods (different fruits, carrot sticks, etc.), something crunchy, and something sweet. Every single day, even on the weekends, Kaz and I eat leftovers, and if there aren't any, we each have a go-to brain-less lunch we repeat day after day.

That approach isn't right for everybody, but it is for us.

Tell the Truth

If you want to Lazy Genius meals, you have to name what you *actually cook*. The ideal world, whatever that looks like for you, is why your kitchen overwhelms you.

For example, our family doesn't eat salad. My kids think anything green is a form of torture, and I don't have the energy to convince them otherwise as I watch the lettuce decompose in the fridge. There-fore, I do not make salad, have salad-related tools, or plan salad as part of our dinners—ever.

Now, would I like to be the mom whose kids slurp up salad like it's a baggie of Goldfish? Obviously. Would I like to be the kind of person who personally eats a lot of salad? Mostly. Salad feels like a Girl Scout Badge of Adulthood. However, I've released the pressure to fit an ideal that doesn't work for me and choose to be lazy about salad in this cur-rent season.

Tell the truth. And that's true, not just for the meals you choose but also for the skills you need to cook them.

Learn How to Get Your Meals on the Table

Do you know how to use a chef's knife and run through all your meal prep, or are you spending extra money on pre-cut vegetables? Pre-cut is fine unless the priority is budget over convenience.

Do you know how to roast or blanch or sauté so that your produce can expand its flavor, or are you mostly eating your vegetables cru-dité style and kind of hating it? Raw is fine unless the priority is flavor over ease.

You need both meals *and skills* that support what matters most. There are so many YouTube videos and kind friends you can ask to show you how to use an Instant Pot or hold a knife or grill a piece of chicken. Also, we haven't even gotten to Part 3 yet, where you'll learn all kinds of things.

Just pay attention to when a skill could help you. Also? Let go of ones that won't.

Here's a personal example. I don't know how to poach a ding-dang thing. Not an egg, not a piece of fish, and not anything else that I can't list, because I don't even know what gets poached. I do know that poaching requires some attention, and we've covered that. *Kendra does not do attention. Kendra does brainless.* By definition, poaching is out for me.

Choose the meals and skills *you* need and get good at them. Don't waste your time trying to know everything when everything doesn't matter.

Step Two
Essentialize
Your Meals

The Objective: Get rid of what's in the way.

Because meal options are basically infinite, you've got to clear the decks. Only keep what serves you right now.

Here are a couple of prime categories to essentialize. If any others come to mind that serve you, go for it. All you're doing is getting rid of what's in the way.

Recipes

Not every recipe is for right now, but cookbooks and food blogs understandably make that hard to remember.

We just love them! They're so pretty and full of food we want to eat!

Remember, food photos are styled to be appealing. If a meal doesn't look good in a photo, you won't want to eat it, and the business is built on your wanting to eat it. That's not a knock on food bloggers; one of my dearest friends is one. It's just how the business works and should! Just remember, you can walk away from a recipe that isn't right for you, even though it's designed to make you want it. You're in charge.

Regarding the actual recipes, remember what matters most about your particular season and weigh your choices of cookbooks and food blogs against it.

Are you focused on inexpensive meals? Don't pick up a cookbook or subscribe to a blog full of expensive specialty ingredients. Are you focused on quick meals? Leave behind resources that love complex recipes with multiple elements.

On the internet, look for bloggers who prioritize what you prioritize. Sometimes it's nice to have one or two websites you can depend on and leave the rest alone.

If you still want to use the Whole Internet, you do you, but under no circumstances should you ever Google "chicken recipes." Friend, that's a sad, endless road going nowhere good. Be specific, based on what matters to you.

Finally, if there are recipes and meals that you *love* but don't make anymore, ask yourself why. It could be they're not for this season, and they'll come back around again. Or it could be because you don't have what you need or you've lost sight of what matters.

Look at your recipes, whether old family favorites or new adventures, through the lens of what matters most *right now*.

Expectations and Comparisons

There are so many expectations and comparisons that are in the way. *So many.*

Where are you holding yourself to ridiculous expectations regarding what you cook? Or that you even cook at all?

The only expectations you should graciously try to meet are the ones *you* set based on what matters most *to you*. Nothing else deserves airtime.

This is why Instagram is so hard. We see curated, styled photos of people having meals that look zero percent like what's on our table, and then we feel exceedingly downtrodden.

Comparison rarely leads us anywhere good, especially when we're comparing our situation to someone who has *different priorities*.

We all get to decide what matters most. You can choose differently than I do and not feel bad about it. Cook what you need to cook. Eat what you need to eat. Delegate what you need to delegate.

As long as your choices support what matters to you, and as long as you offer grace to yourself and to others for choosing differently, you'll enjoy your kitchen.

Now that you have only what you need, let's organize it.

Step Three
Organize
Your Meals

The Objective: Put everything in its place.

This is going to be *fun*.

Here's where we've gotten recipes wrong. We think of them as individuals, that they're all unique and beautiful and have nothing to do with each other. Make this thing, and you're done. Make this other thing, and you're done.

The way we approach recipes is as if they're government spies unwilling to share any information. We don't let our recipes talk to each other and share how they're alike. We haven't yet noticed that recipes are the same general instructions in the same general order, just using different ingredients.

We're going to organize your meals into categories of how they're *made*, not what they are. It's **organizing by type**, and I can't wait to teach you the types.

Real Quick, Though . . .

Let me say this before we get started: "meat and three" is killing you. The expectation that every meal needs to have a main course of meat and three sides is unsustainable. I'm just shooting you straight.

I've heard from hundreds upon *hundreds* of you over the last few years about how your partner grew up with a mom who cooked "meat and three" every meal, so that's what he or she expects from you.

It's time for a come-to-Jesus conversation.

Now listen, if you and your partner decide *together* to prioritize "meat and three" as what matters most in your meals, go for it. But you also have to talk about what you're willing to trade for it.

You will trade time; other tasks will have to get dropped or delegated. You will trade money; sustaining variety across consistent "meat and three" meals will definitely cost something. You will trade responsibility (and in this case, I mean literally trade)—one person cooks, the other cleans up.

However, if that way of eating doesn't matter most, let go of the expectation that every meal must have multiple components. *It does not*. It's time for me to hold your beautiful face again and tell you in my best big-sister voice that you do not have to cook dinner like you're Martha Stewart. [whispers] *You do not have to cook dinner like you're Martha Stewart.*

Okay, now let's start talking about organizing your meals for real.

You Know More Than You Think You Do

When you walk into your kitchen needing to make dinner, you want to know what you're doing. You want confidence. You want to know what's going to end up on the plate after an hour.

But what if you only know how to make, like, ten things, and you're so *tired* of those ten things?

Guess what?

You know how to cook *way more* than you think you do.

Can you cook a taco filling? If so, you can cook a million more things.

Can you cook a meat sauce? If so, you can cook a million more things.

Can you make soup? Any soup in the universe of soups? If so, you can cook a million more things.

So many recipes are carbon copies of each other.

You just need to know what you're looking for.

Welcome to the Liquid Index.

The Liquid Index

Can we just take a moment? My discovery of the Liquid Index felt like finding the Holy Grail. It is a *treasure,* and now I finally get to tell you about it.

The Liquid Index is a customizable recipe blueprint by which you follow the same steps each time but have wildly different results, based on (a) the ingredients you choose and (b) how much liquid you use.

Mostly it's the liquid, hence the name the Liquid Index.

If you understand the Liquid Index, you will never run out of recipes. Like, ever. See The Liquid Index Ingredient Guide on page 158 for ideas.

Here's how it works.

1. **Start with aromatics and bite-sized protein** sautéed in fat and seasoned with salt and any other herbs or spices. Aromatics are things like onions, ginger, and celery, and proteins are meat, fish, beans, tofu, and more. Don't worry; there's a full ingredient list on page 158.
2. **Add bulk** with ingredients like beans, potatoes, and all sorts of other vegetables. Once again, there's a full ingredient list of "bulk" foods on page 158.
3. **Add liquid.**

Let's stop here, since this is where the Liquid Index embraces possibility.

The question you have to ask is: Will you add *a lot* of liquid, *some* liquid, or *no* liquid?

A lot = "soup"
Some = "stew"
None = "sauté"

Those are the three *types* of meals that come out of the Liquid Index, all based simply on how much liquid you add.

Let's go back to that taco filling again. Taco filling—ground beef sautéed with onions and bell peppers—is a "sauté" on the Liquid Index. You can put it in your taco or in your burrito and be good.

But what if you add *some* liquid? One or two cans of crushed tomatoes turns that taco filling (a sauté) into a Mexican-inspired meat sauce (a stew).

Or what if you add *a lot* of liquid? A box of chicken stock along with those crushed tomatoes and a can of green chilis turns that Mexican meat sauce into taco soup.

Hang with me. There's more.

You can choose your own adventure even more because all three types—sauté, stew, and soup—will be eaten *on* something, *in* something, or *alone*.

On flatbread. In a hollowed-out zucchini. On rice. In a bread bowl.

Organizing your meals this way is a lifelong transformative thing. Suddenly you don't have to skip recipes that sound too complicated ("that's a stew on polenta!"), and you have a framework for the recipes you already do well.

You've been sitting on a recipe goldmine and didn't even know it.

So again,

1. Start with sautéed aromatics and bite-sized protein.
2. Add bulk.
3. Add liquid: none for a sauté, some for a stew, or a lot for a soup.
4. Put that in something, on something, or serve it alone.

I want to show you some detailed Liquid Index action, but before I do, I need to tell you about two more things: toppings and flavor.

Toppings are, well, toppings.

You can top sautés, stews, and soups with all kinds of things—herbs, cheese, nuts, sauce, etc. Toppings can add texture, color, or flavor.

Let's talk about **flavor**.

You can add flavor anywhere in the Liquid Index process:

- Add spices when you're cooking the aromatics and protein.
- Add flavorful ingredients like roasted vegetables or chorizo to add bulk.
- Add flavor with liquids in the form of curry paste, chipotle peppers, sun-dried tomatoes, wine, or rich stock.
- Add flavor in the topping.
- *Or all of the above.*

You need flavor, and you can add it at any time.

Okay, let's take a handful of ingredients and watch the Liquid Index open up this recipe wonderland.

The Liquid Index in Action

PORK   +   GARLIC   +   ONION

Rosemary			Cumin	
Roasted Mushrooms	Raw Potato Chunks		No Bulk	Raw Potato Diced
Canned Crushed Tomatoes	Canned Crushed Tomatoes and a Lot of Chicken Stock	A lot of Chicken Stock	No Liquid	Some Chicken Stock and Chipotles
on Polenta	alone	alone	on Tortilla Chips for Nachos	in Burritos
Pork Mushroom Ragu on Cheesy Polenta (topped with fresh parsley)	Hearty Italian Pork Soup (topped with toasted pinenuts and fresh parsley)	Rosemary Potato Pork Soup (topped with Parmesan)	Cumin Pork Oven Nachos (topped with cheese and pickled jalapeños)	Spicy Pork and Potato Burrito
STEW	SOUP	SOUP	SAUTÉ	STEW

Look at those recipe names. They sound kind of familiar, don't they?

That's because so many recipes are built the same way, and chances are you already know how to cook the three types of recipes . . . which means you can cook so much more than you think.

How to Organize Your Meals by the Liquid Index

When you're flipping through a cookbook or scrolling through a food blog, don't dismiss a recipe simply because of the title. Instead, first try to name if it's a sauté, stew, or soup.

It's likely you skipped the recipe because an ingredient in the title isn't beloved in your house. But since you know the Liquid Index, you can name what kind of recipe it is (soup, stew, or sauté). You can see what it's served on, in, or if it's on its own. You can see when the writer added flavor and if they added a topping.

Because you know the Liquid Index, you can make ingredient substitutions and not freak out. You can punch up the flavor if it sounds too bland. You can skip the topping if it seems too complicated and add flavor during a different step.

Once you see it, you will see it everywhere, and it will change your life.

Your recipes aren't government spies anymore! No more individualistic recipes.

Don't forget. There's a fantastic guide to the Liquid Index with the ingredient lists and all the details on page 158.

Always Organize Your Own Way

Obviously, I'm a huge fan of the Liquid Index and *not* a fan of "meat and three" meals, which calls for making four recipes at once, so organizing my meals this way is my go-to.

But it doesn't have to be yours.

You can still organize your recipes based on ingredient, cooking method, or how much time something takes.

But a common problem with organizing your recipes into, say, a "chicken" category is that the only common thread is the chicken. One meal might take twenty minutes while another takes four hours. One meal could have a ton of prep and another none at all.

Once you prioritize what matters most and clear out everything that's in the way, you can put your meals and recipes into their places however you need to.

You might have come into this section thinking I'd share how to organize your actual recipes, like on Evernote or Paprika or index cards. While that is a helpful conversation, I think we get distracted by *where we store the recipes* and forget about *how they're made*. Once you change your thinking about how recipes are put together, you'll probably feel the need to change how you store them, anyway.

But no matter what I find helpful, do what matters most to you. Always.

Now let's personalize your meals.

Step Four
Personalize Your Meals

The Objective: Feel like yourself.

It's easy to feel like a fraud when you cook your meals, and if you feel like a fraud, you *for sure* do not feel like yourself.

When you think about The Seven P's, I think the most important to start with are **people**, **proficiency**, and **pleasure**.

If you cook for other **people**, their **pleasure** is probably tied to yours. If my kids complain about a meal I find delicious, it's hard to not be annoyed or even deeply hurt. How can I avoid that hurt? We can have a House Rule (LGP #6) to use kind words about a meal because it's loving to let others enjoy what they enjoy.

If you're not **proficient** at knowing when food is cooked through, you will super dupe not experience much **pleasure** while cooking, because you're so stressed out your chicken is going to kill somebody. Go buy an instant-read thermometer, chill out, and feel like yourself again.

If you want to feel like yourself when you cook and eat, consider your people, your proficiency, your pleasure, and any of the other Seven P's you want. Start small (LGP #2) with any changes that will make you feel more like yourself.

You don't have to cook like a celebrity chef . . . unless that matters to you.

You don't have to garnish food . . . unless that matters to you.

You don't have to make sides . . . unless that matters to you.

You don't have to know how to cook everything. (I'm just going to stop that one right there.)

Do whatever helps you feel more like yourself in the kitchen. It's yours, and you belong there.

Step Five
Systemize
Your Meals

The Objective: Stay in the flow.

Let's talk about cooking rhythm.

When you walk into the kitchen to make breakfast, lunch, or dinner, you want to feel like you're walking into a room that's ready for you.

We've taken care of some of that by Lazy Geniusing your space, and we hope you feel more confident cooking your meals with the Liquid Index.

Here are some Lazy Genius principles that can help you nail your cooking rhythm even more.

Principal
Picks for
Your Meals

Ask the Magic Question (LGP #3)

"What can I do now to make dinner easier later?"

This question is indeed magic. Ask it any time of day when you have an extra minute or two and see how it transforms your cooking flow.

If you have a couple minutes in the middle of the day, you can make a salad dressing or marinade (a guide for that is on page 151). You can chop the onion. You can season the chicken early. You can fill a pasta pot with water and put it on the stove.

The Magic Question is my favorite way to enjoy a cooking rhythm. A list of ready-to-go answers is on page 183.

Go in the Right Order (LGP #11)

The Liquid Index is already in the right order. Have fun being creative with it.

Beyond that, take a beat to think about what part of your meal takes the longest, and do that thing first or even way in advance. It really helps.

Start Small (LGP #2)

You don't have to overhaul your kitchen or your recipes to enjoy cooking more than you do now. It might just take an apron you love, a playlist that makes you smile or dance, a pot that works well, or a window that you always forget to open but pours in sunlight that makes you take a deep breath.

Live in the Season (LGP #4)

This might be a season of starting dinner an hour earlier than you normally would in anticipation of being interrupted seventeen times by the tiny humans.

This might be a season of eating dinner food for lunch and lunch food for dinner because of competing schedules and energies.

This might be a season of cooking dinner in the morning before the day begins and reading and drinking tea at the end.

Sometimes things feel upside down because we're not letting our season teach us what we need to know. If you pay attention to what's different and *orient* yourself to it rather than *resist* it, your rhythm will feel good to you.

Set House Rules (LGP #6)

Figure out what rules you want to adopt, such as:

The cook picks the music.
The cook doesn't clean up.
Everyone helps with one part of the meal.
No more using extra bowls.

For real, though, on this one. I give you permission to stop using extra bowls. Keep all your prep on a big cutting board. Serve all your taco toppings on a sheet pan covered in parchment paper. Have people portion their plates directly from the pots and pans on the stove. *Why are we using so many bowls?*

Remember the Path for Your Meals

First, *prioritize*. What matters most about how you cook and what you eat in this season of life? Try not to look beyond what's happening now.

Second, *essentialize*. When you know what matters most, you know what meals fit your season and what skills you need to make them. Get rid of everything that's in the way of that, both recipes and ridiculous expectations.

Third, *organize*. Choose meals and ingredients that fit your life right now. Use the Liquid Index to simplify the process.

Fourth, *personalize*. Be yourself in how you cook the meals you choose and give yourself permission to learn however slowly you need to.

Fifth, *systemize*. Pay attention to the rhythm in your kitchen. Go in the right order. Start small with what makes sense. Be kind to yourself as you find your way and use Lazy Genius principles to smooth the edges when things get bumpy.

Now, let's figure out how to plan what you're going to eat without turning into a robot.

plan

How you decide what to eat

Meal planning as a phrase is such a buzzkill for a lot of people. It's loaded with images of intense organization, spreadsheets, and inflexibility.

Intuitively, you probably agree that knowing what's for dinner makes the rest of the day easier, but all the rest of the meal planning stuff has made you tap out. There are few things that so deeply personify the extremes of Lazy and Genius than meal planning. Neither is great, friend!

Stuck in the Genius Way

As a supposed Genius, you must know everything you're going to eat for literally ever.

You have calendars, color-coded recipe labels, spreadsheets with recipes, apps for shopping lists, and a general attitude of superiority that's really masking your fear that it'll all fall apart any minute.

If you picked chicken tacos for Tuesday and you're stuck in the Genius mindset, you're having chicken tacos on Tuesdays. You cannot change your mind just because you want to and then throw the entire plan off its axis.

That's a lot of pressure.

Stuck in the Lazy Way

As a Lazy person, you give up on planning completely, you make what you make whenever you figure it out, and everyone just needs to calm down.

However, on the inside, you are anything but calm because you never know what you're cooking next, and everyone is always hungry. Thank goodness there's lots of room in the middle.

The Lazy Genius Way

The Lazy Genius Way has so much freedom in that middle place:

- You don't feel the pressure to plan everything to the letter.
- You know what planning strategies work for you and leave the others behind.
- You throw away less food, take fewer trips to the store, and depend on convenience in a purposeful way.
- You generally know what you're going to eat next, and when you don't, you have a dependable strategy to figure it out.

Let's take meal planning through our five Lazy Genius steps:

1. **prioritize:** name what matters

2. **essentialize:** get rid of what's in the way

3. **organize:** put everything in its place

4. **personalize:** feel like yourself

5. **systemize:** stay in the flow

Whenever your meal planning game just cannot score, come back to these five steps. They will never fail you.

Step One
Prioritize
Your Plan

The Objective: Name what matters most.

If everything matters about planning, you will never plan. That's just a fact. Or you'll try, do it poorly, and give up in the end anyway.

If you've already given up on meal planning altogether, please take a minute to scrap your current paradigm so we can start fresh. I promise you don't have to do it "that way" for it to work. You just have to know what matters most to you, and I'll show you how to plan with that in mind.

What *Could* Matter About Your Plan?

You're in charge here. Let your own life be the guiding force in what could matter, but use this list as a place to start. As you read, pay attention to what has you nodding in agreement.

- **Simplicity:** Create a plan in as few steps as possible.
- **Frequency:** Plan often, rarely, or somewhere in between, but your preferred frequency steers the ship.
- **Shopping:** You only have one chunk of time to shop, so your planning has to connect with whenever that is.
- **Energy:** You don't want to feel stressed out at mealtimes or during the actual planning,
- **Meal:** One of the three daily meals gives you a lot of trouble, so focusing on that specific meal is important.
- **Analog vs. Digital:** Embracing one wholeheartedly might be necessary for the plan to happen at all.
- **Communal:** The whole family is part of the process.
- **Ease:** Even if there are a few extra steps, they're all easy and don't require much brainpower from you or whoever else is planning.
- **Time Frame:** You like the idea of meal planning either one or two days at a time, up to an entire month or two, or somewhere in between.

Got any more? Jot them down.

What *Does* Matter About Your Plan?

Remember, live in your season. You want to narrow the list down to two or three things that matter *right now*. No ideals, no futures, no "when this changes." Right. Now.

The priorities you leave behind aren't priorities anymore. Maybe they're considerations, but they don't get to have a say in how you plan. Choose what will keep having a say, and you'll know how to plan your meals in a helpful, personal way.

A quick note: your priorities could be *how* you plan, *what* you plan, or *when* you plan. Pay attention to which category gives you the most energy as you narrow down what matters.

What Matters *Most* About Your Plan?

If you're having trouble naming which of your three picks gets top billing, play around with a couple of scenarios with different priorities to see which one feels right. Imagination always helps you narrow things down.

This next perspective might help, too.

What matters most to me is ease, and that can look different at any given time. Sometimes ease is thinking ahead and planning the whole month, and sometimes ease is going from meal to meal and feeling okay in picking spaghetti again.

My actual planning *strategy* isn't the point. In fact, it changes often. But as long as it's *easy*, I'm in.

Let that free you up. Knowing what matters most doesn't automatically determine the system; the systems can change *around* what matters most.

Have What You Need for Your Plan

Now that you've done some thinking, do you have all you need to plan? Are there things you're missing? Tangible resources? Time? Help? Energy?

Think about what you need. If you don't have it, figure out a way to get it.

Now that you know what matters most, you're going to get rid of what's in the way.

Step Two
Essentialize
Your Plan

The Objective: Get rid of what's in the way.

When you get rid of what doesn't matter, you can more easily see what does matter or where you have gaps to fill. Be ruthless. Here are some elements of your plan that might need some attention.

Apps

Pull out your smartphone. Do you have any apps for planning? List makers, task keepers, recipe storers, etc.?

Delete what overwhelms you. Chances are you've downloaded a handful of possible planning helpers, and all they do is clog up your phone and dampen your confidence.

If you're an app hoarder or you think you might use the apps again one day, put the not-right-now apps in a folder in the back, and leave them there until you need them again.

Systems, Binders, and Lists

Do you have a handful of ebooks or printables that are on your computer or printed out in your kitchen, untouched and in the way? Do you have seventeen Pinterest boards taunting you with other people's meal plans that don't fit your priorities?

If you're not using something, it likely doesn't work for you right now. If you're wondering if it *will work*, take the time to find out. Explore that system or run it past the lens of what matters most to you. Does it support that? If it doesn't, let it go.

Also, I know it's hard when you have paid for a system you didn't use. Maybe if you give it just one more try! Even though the other four tries were a bust! *It's okay.* Some things are an investment in what *doesn't* work.

Planning Rhythms

Just because you've always planned one way, that doesn't mean it's the *only* way. There are other options.

Pay attention to your current planning rhythms (even if that rhythm is deciding twenty minutes before you start making food) and get rid of any routines or rhythms that don't work anymore. Maybe you're used to pulling out a stack of cookbooks on Sunday night and making your list, only now you have two kids under two years old and you currently don't know what day of the week it is.

Get rid of what isn't serving you, even things as intangible as *when* you make a choice.

Expectations

The chances are sky high that you have unreasonable expectations for yourself on how planning should be. Cut that junk out right now.

Telling yourself a meal plan only counts if it looks a certain way, especially when that way supports something that doesn't matter to you, makes zero sense. Yet you still do it.

Ask yourself what expectations you have of meal planning and which ones are getting in the way. If it helps, put a new expectation or bit of permission in its place. Create a new meal-planning mantra that shines a spotlight on what matters most.

For example, a couple of years ago, I shared a weekly meal plan on Instagram, and there were three or four nights in a row of chicken. So many people were, like, "Wait, you're having SO MUCH CHICKEN! Isn't your family mad about that?!" It was as if I missed the Chicken Rule that everyone else knew already. But guess what? We like chicken. We don't eat fish. Beef is expensive. It's fine!

If you have expectations, like you can't have chicken two nights in a row, ask yourself *why* you think that, especially up against what matters most. It might be you're hamstringing yourself in service of an arbitrary rule that doesn't fit your life anyway.

Well done on essentializing! Now let's organize what's left.

Step Three
Organize Your Plan

The Objective: Put everything in its place.

This is a bold claim, but I'm going to say it anyway: my superpower is organizing and systemizing meal planning. If you're new to the Lazy Genius way of things, you're about to "have your brain blowed," as my daughter used to say when she was tiny.

I've been waiting so patiently for this part, and now the *floodgates*.

Organize Your Plan by Type

Planning your meals involves choosing a small number of ideas from a larger number of ideas, right? You have a selection of recipes, and then you pick some to cover a certain period of time.

This is obviously basic, but sometimes naming the essence of something helps us see it more clearly.

If you're pulling meal ideas from somewhere—a Pinterest board, a cookbook, a stack of written recipe cards, your brain—it's tremendously helpful to organize those choices and view where they come from through the lens of what matters to you.

Here are some ideas of what I mean . . .

Brainless Crowd-Pleasers

This is a magic way to plan for everyone, no matter what matters to you.

A brainless crowd-pleaser, which I will call a BCP from now on, is a meal that **takes very little brainpower to cook** and **is generally pleasing to the people who eat it**.

The good news? Every recipe on the planet could be brainless and a crowd-pleaser for someone, somewhere. This doesn't have to mean just red and brown foods that come out of a jar or a box. They can! But they don't have to.

So, think through the meals you often make and write down what qualifies as a BCP for the people living in your home. You might have one, you might have twenty-one. There's no magic number, so just take what you have and be grateful for it.

Gather your own BCPs, list them somewhere together, and choose from that limited selection whenever you need to.

Plan B Meals

Emergency scenarios are plentiful.

You grab the chicken you were going to cook, and it smells like death. Soccer practice runs late. You forgot to plug in the slow cooker. A recipe is just a total inedible bust. You just got home, and everyone is hungry *now*.

It happens to everyone and more often than you think. That's why a list of meals that can save an emergency is a great way to organize your plan. A plan is simply a way to choose something on purpose a tiny bit ahead of time, and sometimes the meal you intended to make no longer fits the time, energy, or ingredients you expected to have. Sometimes Plan A just doesn't happen.

So have a list of Plan B meals.

Cereal, sandwiches, flatbread pizzas, microwave quesadillas, a usual takeout order from a favorite place so you don't have to wonder what everyone wants. Yes, it feels weird and redundant to write down "cereal" in a list of Plan B meals. Isn't cereal by nature a Plan B choice? But in stressful situations, your brain thinks, "It's been fun, fam, but I'm OUT." It's harder to make choices under stress, and especially at the end of the day.

Help your brain by writing down your Plan B meals, even it feels silly.

Clock Meals

Clock Meals are ones that are built around time. I mean, yeah, every meal is built around time, but if time is a priority for you, creating a list with that focus will help.

If you work full time out of the house, you need a dinner that can be made quickly *or* was started before you left. Maybe your Clock Meal list is a collection of slow-cooker meals, previously prepped meals that need just a quick spin in a skillet, or meals where the food marinates in the fridge all day and then you roast it when you get home.

(A lot of newer ovens have a timer option for preheating, so see if yours does; it makes it easy to have a hot oven when you get home.)

If time started and time spent are important, Clock Meals will save your life.

Last Call Ideas

You are smart and can for sure come up with your own ways to organize your plan, but in case you're tired, here are some rapid-fire ideas to help you out.

- **Crowd Meals:** For your teenage son's group of friends, your church community group, your book club, your parties, your meal shares with other families
- **Celebration Meals:** Special, fun, favorite meals your people love
- **Budget Meals:** Meals that cost less than a certain amount, for when money is tight
- **Delegation Meals:** Meals with steps that are easy enough for a non-cook to do
- **Reset Meals:** Meals that get your body back to a good place after days of eating your kid's sandwich crusts
- **Bucket List Meals:** Specific things you want to cook at some point in your life

Organize Your Plan by Task

Planning based on specific *types* of meals might work well for you, but some people would rather organize their plan by the *tasks* required of the meal. If that might be you, read on.

You might prefer thinking about meals in terms of *how* they are made. Organize by the cooking vessel or technique: Instant Pot meals, slow-cooker meals, sheet-pan meals, one-pot meals, big-skillet meals, the Liquid Index, etc. When it's time to make a plan, you know what task best suits the day you're planning for, and you have a recipe list organized by that particular task.

A final word on organization: there will be overlap, so don't assume your organization is wrong because one meal can go into three groups or even that one entire group overlaps another group. The point is to make planning work for you, so however that needs to look, overlap or not, go for it.

Now let's make the plan your own.

Step Four
Personalize
Your Plan

The Objective: Feel like yourself.

You do not have to meal-plan the way the internet tells you to for it to count as a plan.

I hope I've already made that clear, but I'll say it again, *just in case*.

You do not have to meal-plan the way *anyone* tells you to. Please just do what works for you.

If you love the **pleasure** of choosing meals from cookbooks, taking your time and flipping pages, do that.

If you love the **process** of meal planning three months at a time, even though other people say you're crazypants, still do it.

If your **personality** needs to listen to Demi Lovato when you open up your Pinterest board so you'll be fierce and motivated, then by all means listen to Demi!

Consider your **people** . . . what they need and how they can help you plan.

Consider your **proficiency**. Are you not naturally organized? Maybe don't create an elaborate binder situation.

Whatever it is, use that thing to make meal planning your own.

Now it's time to blow your mind with a meal-planning rhythm.

Step Five
Systemize
Your Plan

The Objective: Stay in the flow.

You could use literally every single Lazy Genius principle to make a meal-planning rhythm. Every single one.

Because we eat so often and bring so many different priorities to the table, every principle can come into play. Flip to page 14 for a reminder of all thirteen principles, but here are some favorites to get you moving.

Principal Picks for Your Plan

Decide Once (LGP #1)

Let me introduce you to the **Meal Matrix**.

A Meal Matrix is a way of deciding just once what type of meal goes on what day, and then all you have to do is plug-and-play. Pasta Monday, Taco Tuesday, Pizza Friday, etc.

Other ways to decide only once include what day you'll plan, how many resources you'll pull from, where your plan will go, and that you will always choose Brainless Crowd-Pleasers on busy/rainy/messy/[fill in the blank] days.

Batch It (LGP #9)

Batching is doing a task just one time, rather than repeating it like you might ordinarily do.

Meal planning itself is batching. You have to choose what you'll eat several times a day, so by choosing several meals at once, you're batching the decision-making.

A more specific way to batch-plan is to create a **Dinner Queue**. If you're in a season of life or a season on the calendar when the same general list of meals will serve you for a while, put them in one Dinner Queue. That's the list you pull from when it's time to plan, and nowhere else. You're essentially taking the entire world of recipes, pulling together a specific batch, and choosing from those—*and only those*—over and over again.

Once your queue stops being helpful, make a different one.

Build the Right Routine (LGP #5)

A meal-planning rhythm is the goal, right? Some kind of dependable regularity, whether that happens every day, once a week, once a month, or whatever interval you want.

If a Lazy Genius routine is built on where you're going more than the specific steps you take to get there, be sure you're naming what you're ultimately after. Then you can slowly build a routine to stay connected to that rhythmic goal.

One thing that helps my rhythm is to ask my family every Sunday night what they'd enjoy eating that coming week. I don't always use every suggestion, but it's helpful to know what they'd like and what they are *liking*. Plus, I don't mind the repetition, since ease is my main goal. Asking them what they want, while often resulting in the same answers, is about as easy as it comes and creates a routine I enjoy.

Build a meal-planning routine around a show you watch, a specific time of day, a day of the week, or anything else that works for you.

Schedule Rest (LGP #12)

This one is important. Build rest into your meal plans.

You don't have to cook every meal. You don't have to *plan* every meal. Pay attention to the point where you grow weary in the meal-planning process, and instead of bucking up and pushing through, maybe schedule some rest instead.

My food buddy, Bri McKoy, knows that on Thursdays, she just fizzles out. Bri is an amazing cook, with a flavor-flexible husband and all the tools and skills she needs, and she *still* fizzles out. It happens to literally the best of us. So, for her, Thursdays are takeout night. Always. She's built in the rest rather than pushing through. This is how to meal-plan like a Lazy Genius.

This is why you should do things your own way . . . so you'll keep doing them!

Remember the Path

First, *prioritize*. Name what matters most about meal planning, and then choose whatever supports that one thing.

Second, *essentialize*. Get rid of all the apps, systems, and expectations that are dragging you down. Leave room for what actually matters.

Third, *organize*. Create some lists of specific meals so planning happens in two minutes rather than two overwhelming hours.

Fourth, *personalize*. Do it the way you do it, and don't feel weird about it. Meal-plan with all the tabs and lists and color-coded stuff, or meal-plan in the grocery store on your way home from work. Whatever works for you deserves a high five. No need to compare.

Fifth, *systemize*. Use the Lazy Genius principles of batching, deciding once, and anything else that works for you to start small and slowly build a rhythm that makes meal planning helpful and enjoyable, not a drag.

Go team. Now that you have a plan for your meals, you need the food to make them. That's next.

food

Choosing, storing +
shopping for ingredients

You're told to have a stocked kitchen, but it's kind of a lie.

I mean, you *can*—and for your priorities, you may even want to—but stocked with *what*?

For too long, we have let other people tell us the answer. We read the lists in the cookbooks and on the food blogs, and suddenly find ourselves buying cans of beans we don't know how to cook and tuna packed in oil (not water, don't be an animal) and, of course, roasted red peppers. Good golly, *the roasted red peppers*.

Every cookbook author tells me to stock roasted red peppers. Every single one. I'm guessing someone hasn't, but I have yet to find that author.

Guess what? I don't like roasted red peppers. At *all*. Maybe if you swirl them in a dip with feta or whatever, I'll try a bite, but I am not a dip person either (don't judge me), and I just don't care.

However, for *years* I bought roasted red peppers because all the people *who love roasted red peppers* told me to do so. Then I had a pantry full of unopened roasted red peppers. Or, there was that time I bought the giant jar at Costco because I thought I should be a grown-up and eat them, and *this was a better deal!* But then I ate only one pepper and found the giant jar covered in four shades of mold months later.

I want to save you from four shades of mold. Otherwise, you're swinging for the fences with all Lazy or all Genius.

Stuck in the Genius Way

You basically stop just short of buying the entire grocery store. You must have every single ingredient "to throw dinner together" in a confident and carefree way.

To organize all these new, magical ingredients, you turn to multiple viewings of *The Home Edit*, splurging on the special clear containers to de-box and label everything. Halfway through the cereal, you realize you don't have enough containers, and you quit.

Three days later, you still can't figure out what's for dinner, you reach for an Oreo to soften the edges on your annoyance, and instead you bump up against tins of Italian anchovies that are quietly laughing at you.

Stuck in the Lazy Way

You buy kale without a plan to cook it because you think you'll figure that out later. You buy chicken because you always eat chicken but forget about the chicken until its smell reminds you that you bought the chicken. You buy stuff that's on sale because it's a good deal and you're sure you'll come up with something.

You stuff produce into the crisper drawer until nothing else fits, finally prompting you to throw away everything that's liquefied in the bottom, just to make room.

Cabinets and pantries remain full of what you don't use, while you keep buying what you don't need or forget to buy what you actually do need.

This is the part in the story where you start storing food in the garage while still ordering pizza because you forgot about the chicken once again.

No more, pal. *No more.*

The Lazy Genius Way

It's a simple way, my friend.

You know the food you like.
You buy the food you need.
You store the food where you can find it.
You ignore the food other people say is important.
You decide what matters.

I don't know why we've been complicating it for so long, but no more. Let's Lazy Genius your food.

As always, we'll use our five steps to get there.

1. **prioritize:** name what matters

2. **essentialize:** get rid of what's in the way

3. **organize:** put everything in its place

4. **personalize:** feel like yourself

5. **systemize:** stay in the flow

Whenever you feel out of rhythm with the food moving in and out of your kitchen, whether you're cooking for one or twenty-one, always come back to these five steps. They will serve you forever.

Let's get started.

Step One Prioritize Your Food

The Objective: Name what matters most.

When it comes to your food, we need to name what matters in three different categories: **ingredients, shopping, and storage.** The three will hit their pinnacle together in the Systemize section of this chapter because you can't enjoy a food rhythm without the food moving in and out of your kitchen.

As always, you'll use these three questions to drill down to your true priorities:

1. What *could* matter?
2. What *does* matter?
3. What matters *most*?

Let's start with ingredients.

INGREDIENTS

What could matter about the ingredients you keep around? There are a lot of factors, some of which I've listed here. Specifically, sometimes the food you keep around depends on what kind of cook you are, so notice those first two bullet points especially.

- **Recipe vs. Riff:** If you only cook from recipes, you only need ingredients the recipes call for. If you like to riff, you'll want a few options to jazz up your meal.

- **Variety vs. Repetition:** If you like variety, you'll probably have extra ingredients that don't get used for a while. If you like repetition, you want to keep your regular ingredients stocked so you always have what you need.

- **Cuisine Preference:** Is there a certain flavor profile you like? Having flavor staples for, say, Thai, Indian, or Greek food would help you have what you need and use what you have.

- **Budget:** You don't have extra money to waste on one-off ingredients, so you focus on reasonably priced ingredients you'll use often. Or, you buy in bulk or when there's a big sale and then you cook from that stockpile accordingly.

- **Nutrition:** If you have any sort of intolerance, sensitivity, allergy, or health issue directly impacted by food, focusing on the nutritional components of your food is what you pay attention to most.

- **Easy Path to Flavor:** A fresh artichoke takes some work to make it good. A box of mac and cheese doesn't. Think about how much work you're willing to put into an ingredient to make it work for you.
- **Convenience:** If you do not have time for excess chopping, mixing, and marinating, foods need to be close to done.
- **Confidence:** You want to know how to cook something without watching four YouTube videos to figure it out.
- **Sustainability:** You want to grow your own food or support local farmers who do.

Narrow down your list to two or three things. Then, as always, choose the one that matters most.

For me, it's confidence. I want to be able to cook any ingredient any number of ways with my eyes closed. Remember, brainless and easy. That's my vibe. Adventurous cooking with new ingredients is not in my near future, and I accept that. Do I always like it? Nah. But I accept it for the sake of what matters most.

And remember, as you think about the foods you have on hand and use, don't be afraid to ignore foods other people swear by. *You get to choose.*

If you don't cook it, it's taking up space, or, worse, rotting in your fridge. Again, we reject all choices that lead to four shades of mold.

SHOPPING

Let's prioritize your shopping next. What could matter, what does matter, and what matters most? This is an area where you'll feel an immediate shift once it's prioritized.

What could matter?

- **Convenience:** The shopping process is easy on your life. Maybe it's shopping at one store instead of four, being able to use grocery pickup, easily stopping on the way home from work, online ordering options, or anything else that isn't a strain.
- **Price:** An obvious one.
- **Selection:** This could include quality, options for dietary restrictions, items being in stock, or a variety across the board. Or the opposite; you might love a store that just sells the basics because you're overwhelmed otherwise.
- **Experience:** Good customer service, lighting, layout, clear display of the ingredients, the produce area being tended to, self-checkouts that actually work.
- **Time:** You want the whole thing to take as little time as possible. Maybe that means shopping at a big-box store with lower prices because you don't have time to cut coupons.

Start narrowing down to what does matter to you, and then choose what matters most.

Remember to **live in your season** as you choose. Life will not always be this way, but while it is, try to embrace it as best you can.

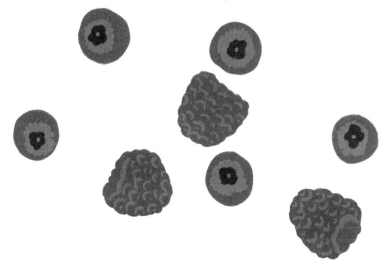

STORAGE

Food storage can be a bear because of the extras and backups, having limited space, or feeling the pressure to have everything perfectly stacked and organized in your pantry . . . or to even have a pantry at all.

You need to prioritize so you can know where to spend your energy and money. Let's narrow it down again. You're getting so good at this.

What could matter?

- **Accessibility:** You can get to everything easily without moving a bunch of stuff around.
- **Consistency:** The same things go in the same places every single time.
- **Aesthetics:** You want it to look pretty.
- **Rotation:** Old stuff always gets used first, and stuff doesn't find the time to expire because you know where it is and use it.
- **Ease:** You can quickly put things away and know where to find them when it's time.

Now what does matter? And what matters *most*? Narrow, narrow, narrow.

Again, your priority *frees you* to know what to do.

Have What You Need

Let's say your priority for both your ingredients and where you shop is **price**. You're on a tight budget, so taking the time to shop sales and go to multiple stores is worth it.

Your storage priority is rotation because you don't want to waste the money you just saved by letting things go bad.

If those are your main food priorities, you can take expensive grocery stores off the table, factor in extra time every week to check sales, and limit your bulk shopping to ingredients you know you'll use so you can store and rotate through what you already have.

If that's the case, when you're at the store and you see a simmer sauce you've been wanting to try that's on sale, don't automatically stock up. Remember, your storage priority is rotation and using what you bought so there's no waste. Is there room for another group of items to rotate through? If there's not, especially if the ingredient is something new, consider which priority is more important: saving the money or storing it so you can see it. Maybe it's better to buy one, try it out, and then make room if you'd like to buy more.

Do not forget this, especially when considering food. It's great to have what you need, but you very much need to use what you have. Buying in bulk and stocking up doesn't help you if you don't use the food.

Now that you know your priorities, it's time to essentialize.

Step Two Essentialize Your Food

The Objective: Get rid of what's in the way.

This will be so gratifying. Let's purge some stuff, and we're going to stick with our three categories: ingredients, shopping, and storage.

Ingredients

When you have twenty minutes, get two big grocery bags. One bag is for trash and the other is for food to give away.

Head to your pantry or the cabinet that holds most of your nonperishable food. Pull out every item you forgot was there, you don't use anymore, has expired, or makes you wonder why you bought it in the first place.

As you go through your stuff, ask if foods are there because you think they're *supposed to be* or if you really need them. If you think you're supposed to stock canned corn but you prefer frozen or don't even like corn, get rid of the canned corn. And then stop buying canned corn.

Do this with everything.

Remember, don't organize yet. Leave what you use where it is. You can organize later.

Now that you see what made it to a bag, it's the perfect time to essentialize your shopping.

Shopping

We're going to ask three questions to help you essentialize your shopping and stop buying stuff you don't need.

First, *why did I buy this?* Look in those essentialized bags as you ask.

If you answer, "I want to eat healthier," but those healthy foods are still sitting there uneaten, maybe you need a different approach *or* need to be honest about your true priority. If the answer is "They were on sale" but you're getting rid of them, you paid for something you didn't use, which is a waste of money no matter how good the deal was.

Notice what you bought that you didn't use, and *stop buying that thing*. You can even make a Don't Buy list on your phone or in your shopping app or wherever you make your list. Writing those items down not only reminds you of them but also keeps you from being seduced by sales.

The second question is *what am I missing?*

If you prioritize a certain cuisine but you don't have the pantry staples to cook a lot of the recipes you want to try, add those ingredients to your shopping list. They're worth it because they matter to you.

And the third question is *do I need to buy this in bulk?* Notice what's well past the "best if used by" date. It could be a food you do cook with but not often enough to buy in bulk. Just because you can buy more at once doesn't mean you need to.

Another reason you're stuck with excessive bulk buys is because you couldn't see them. That's storage, and it comes next.

Storage

The whole point of a Lazy Genius kitchen is to have what you need and use what you have.

You might buy something in bulk because you need it, but if you can't *see it* because of your storage situation, you won't use it. Bummer.

To essentialize your storage, get rid of any systems, gadgets, bins, or baskets that are in the way of what matters.

Do you have big see-through bins that look pretty but aren't practical and you'd rather have practical? Get rid of them.

Do you need a better way to see your cans because you just threw so many away? Get a Lazy Susan or some other kind of can storage.

Are you storing the kids' instant oatmeal packets on the top shelf of the cabinet because that's the only place left, but since the kids can't reach them, the same oatmeal has been there since your kinder-gartener was born? Store them somewhere else.

You know these things without my having to tell you. You're a very smart person. But sometimes we get so busy and so used to the way things are that we forget we can do something different. Essentialize your cabinets, your pantry, and your shopping habits by viewing them through that lens. Get rid of what's in the way of what matters. You'll feel so much better. And we haven't even organized yet!

That's up next.

Step Three Organize Your Food

The Objective: Put everything in its place.

Before you organize by zone, remember that the first zone is your broadest category, the outer layer of your Russian nesting doll. Consider your cabinets, pantries, closets, garage, fridge, freezer, and even your shopping list. It could be that somewhere in there, thinking in zones will help you organize in a way that supports what matters most.

Your Shopping List

You've heard this idea before, but your shopping list tends to work out well when it's organized by zone—that is, where the stuff is in the store. It's harder to miss something when the items are generally close together as you walk the aisles.

A Kid Zone

If what matters most is that your kids can get the food they need without asking, think about organizing a part of your kitchen as a Kid Zone.

In the pantry—probably in the bottom half, depending on the height of your tiny humans—have breakfast foods, agreed-upon snacks, and dinners they know how to start themselves. I grew up amid so many families that stored cereal in the very top cabinet, and no one could ever reach it. Which, I suppose, could've been the point in some cases? Frosted Flakes are incredible and can lead to understandable glut-tony, but you might store something somewhere because that's where your mom put it. You can choose differently if you need to.

A Baking Zone

Flour, sugar, leaveners, chocolate chips, and all the other baking things can go in one place. When it's time to bake, you're not opening a million cabinets.

However, when you're working out a zone, don't assume you have to fit every last possible item in that one place.

For example, I have a Baking Zone, but in three different places. I have a shelving unit in my kitchen for all my glass jars that hold flours and sugar, as well as my pretty Dutch ovens. If they look nice, why not leave them out in plain view? That's a zone on display. Then the bottom of my kitchen pantry is for all the other baking things—chocolate chips, brown sugar, nuts, sprinkles, and the little bits and bobs that are needed. That's a zone with immediate access. Then in my closet pantry down the hall, I have one main shelf for all the backup baking supplies. That's the zone for my extras.

Zones can exist in multiple storage areas and still work great.

A Can Is Not a Zone

You have a lot of cans, right? And they're probably stored in the same place, right? That's understandable. Everyone does it. I'd like to offer a better way—that is, organizing by task. But please do not let the shape of your food become an accidental zone.

You think that organizing by size and shape is a good idea, but doing that *first* is going in the wrong order.

Too many things exist in cans, and mindlessly stacking corn, sweetened condensed milk, diced tomatoes, green chile peppers, tuna, and Beanie Weenees in the same space just because they're in a can is unsustainable.

Do not create a zone based on the size and shape of your food. It won't work. I will not boss you very often, but this is not one of those times. The boss is here. *Do not organize by shape and size.*

Here's another way you can. *Can? Get it?* I'll show myself out.

Organize by Task

Task is your next level, the middle nesting doll. Think about organizing your food based on *what* you're cooking.

Cuisine

This is a fun one that might give you some great structure in your pantry especially.

The nonperishable foods stored in my actual kitchen are snacks, lunch stuff for the kids, and oils and spices for cooking. Everything else—the canned tomatoes, pasta, rice, all of it—is in a closet down the hall. For me, I'd rather walk a few extra steps and have what I need than cram everything into the kitchen.

Within my pantry closet, I organize by the task of *what I'm cooking*. There's a shelf that's all Asian-related ingredients—soba and ramen noodles, curry packets, jars of chili paste and simmer sauces, and cans of coconut milk. I have another shelf that's all canned tomatoes and pasta.

Now, do I use tomatoes in Asian dishes, like chicken tikka masala? Yes. Some ingredients will obviously overlap, but I like pairing things up with their most obvious partners based on the task, on what I'm cooking. Then it's easy to grab everything I need when it's all next to each other.

Lunch

You might currently have the bread in one spot, the ham and cheese in the deli drawer, the lettuce in the crisper drawer, and the mayo and mustard on the door. That's actually where all of my stuff currently is.

But what if pulling all that out from different places makes you crazy? What if what matters most is limited movements and efficiency? Then put all the sandwich stuff on one shelf or in its own bin and organize by the task of making a sandwich.

It all depends on what matters most to *you*.

Organize by Type

Type is the tiniest, most specific part, the itty-bitty inside nesting doll.

You will likely organize by type within a zone or task. For example, on my Asian Dinner Shelf, all the coconut milk is stacked together. On the Tomato Pasta shelf, all the spaghetti boxes are together next to all the macaroni, next to all the diced tomatoes, and so on.

Here are some other ways to think about it.

The Freezer

Your freezer needs organization and fast. Most of us just throw bags and boxes in there and hope for the best.

I promise there's a better way.

You don't have to label everything or have a freezer list taped up somewhere (although you can and should, if knowing what's in there matters most), but if you organize by type within the freezer itself, you'll find stuff more easily.

Maybe all the bagged vegetables go in one drawer, stuff for smoothies in another. Ice cream goes on this shelf. Meat goes on that one.

Think about the type of food or meal and organize your food loosely in there. You might have to do some digging, but at least you're digging through one drawer as opposed to the entire freezer.

The Fridge

The door of your fridge is likely a Sauce Condiment Zone already. Within that zone, you could organize by type—hot sauces together, sandwich stuff together, salad dressings together.

Again, you likely do this to a point already, but sometimes a little extra intention around what matters takes organization to a more sustainable, enjoyable place.

Lead with what matters, put everything in its place, and you'll have what you need, use what you have, and enjoy it.

Now let's make sure you feel like yourself in the process.

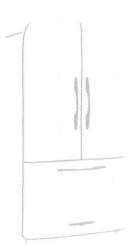

Step Four
Personalize
Your Food

The Objective: Feel like yourself.

You can choose, shop for, and store your food in a way that's personal. There is not one pantry list, one shopping rhythm, or one way to store everything once it's home. You can feel like yourself even in those seemingly standard choices.

You don't have to coupon. If saving money is not a priority, stop looking through coupons. That's not part of your **process.**

If you get a freakish amount of **pleasure** from hot sauce, make space for all the hot sauces. Fill a whole shelf with them because *they matter.*

If organizing your groceries in an orderly way brings you **peace,** buy the containers and shelves without apology.

If your **personality** doesn't do well with crowds, try to find a time to shop when the store is quieter, or put in earbuds (you're not being antisocial) and listen to something you love.

P.S.: If you don't like roasted red peppers, stop buying roasted red peppers.

Simplicity and minimalism aren't the goal. The goal is to have what you need, use what you have, and enjoy it. *You get to decide what that is.*

Now we keep the flow going.

Step Five
Systemize
Your Food

The Objective: Stay in the flow.

A rhythm is trying to take shape here, if it hasn't already. There's natural movement to bringing food in and out of your kitchen as you shop and eat, so applying a few well-chosen Lazy Genius principles will make it flow even better.

Principal Picks for Your Food

Decide Once (LGP #1)

Remember, deciding once is simply making one decision and never thinking about it again.

You can decide once . . .

- what ingredients you will or will not buy for this season in your life
- where you will shop
- the day you will shop
- how often you will shop
- where everything goes and stick with it

My aforementioned friend, Bri McKoy, decided once where she will buy meat. Flavor matters the most to her, and quality is a close second. Therefore, she gets all her meat delivered to her house from a subscription service that has high-quality, high-flavor meats, and it has transformed her energy around cooking.

Broken record alert: limits are not bad. Limits give you freedom. Set one that makes sense for you.

Build the Right Routine (LGP #5)

When you run out of something, it helps to have an existing place to write down what you need to buy. Maybe it's a dry erase board in your kitchen, an app on your phone, or the online grocery cart that's waiting for your next curbside order. That's a routine. You want to know what to buy when you go shopping, so you create an easy on-ramp to remember by having a single place you keep your list.

When you get home from the store, put the food where it goes. Don't leave it on the floor of the pantry in the bag and assume you'll "put it away later." You won't. You never do. Neither do I. Remember, you start a routine with where you want to go, and if you want to go to a place of knowing where everything is and not tripping over packed bags, build a routine of putting stuff in its place *first* so you can experience that feeling of calm in your kitchen.

If you want a calmer cooking experience, having all your food close by can help. So, when you start to cook, think to yourself, "I'm going to get everything I need now so I'm not running around the kitchen looking for things for the next half hour." Make that gathering of ingredients a routine.

Live in the Season (LGP #4)

This is a big one, per usual.

You are always in a season for certain things and not for others. It could be the season for trimming the budget or accepting the cost of convenience. It could be the season for eating a limited number of foods or exploring and learning from every aisle. It could be the season of stocking up or saving space. It could be the season to go to the store every day because you need something to do with your baby or to only buy food that someone else picked out for you.

Live in your season. Knowing it won't always be this way helps you not resent where you are.

Set House Rules (LGP #6)

House Rules are set rules to follow to keep you from losing sight of what matters before things spin out of control.

Here are some ideas:

- I will not buy ingredients I don't have a plan for.
- I will buy prewashed greens so they do not rot waiting to be washed.
- My counters will be cleared *before* I leave for a shopping trip so that everything has a place to easily land when I get home.
- Reusable shopping bags are returned to the car after groceries are put away.
- New stuff goes in the back.
- Whoever finishes a food item writes it on the shopping list.

Use any principles you like, always viewing them through the lens of what matters most.

Remember the Path

First, *prioritize*. Name what matters most about the food you keep in your home, how you shop for it, and how you store it.

Second, *essentialize*. Get rid of foods and choices that are in the way. Notice what keeps expiring, what's been in the back of your cabinet since you moved into your house three years ago, and what no one ever eats. Get rid of what isn't working to make room for what does.

Third, *organize*. Put everything in its place by zone, task, or type. You make the rules.

Fourth, *personalize*. Eat what matters. Shop where it matters. Store food how it matters. Have an entire freezer filled with ice cream and not a prepped meal in sight, or only eat prepped meals from the freezer. Do whatever makes you feel like yourself.

Fifth, *systemize*. Apply any Lazy Genius principle to how you make your shopping list, go to the store, or get food out when it's time to eat. Pay attention to your own rhythm, and when it feels clunky, apply a principle.

The point? *You do you.*

You're doing so great! This is so fun! Prep is up next.

prep

Getting your kitchen
ready for later

They say the kitchen is the heart of the home. Prep is how you keep it from going into cardiac arrest.

When I say prep, the idea is so much bigger than sliced veggies, lunch kits, and meal plans. Prep is the steady pulse of your kitchen. It's a rhythmic stability that upholds what really matters.

Think about the natural rhythm of your meals: early morning coffee, breakfast, lunch, an afternoon snack, dinner, an after-dinner snack, and back again. (Middle-earth hobbits obviously had a much longer list than this.)

Your natural rhythm might be a bit different from mine, but the idea is generally the same for everyone. If there is a natural rhythm to our meals, it makes sense that there is a natural rhythm to *how we prepare them*.

But we often ignore that rhythm in pursuit of being all lazy or all genius. You know this already, reader. Neither one is a good call.

Stuck in the Genius Way

If you're stuck in the Genius Way, the fridge is always stocked with ready-to-go foods. You have multiple bento boxes of cooked lunches, containers of prepped vegetables for snacks and dinner, and home-made cold brew and kombucha getting happy, too.

You have long, well-organized cooking days to stock up on freezer meals. You always have a second use for leftovers, and you'd better believe it's creative. You always follow your plan and never have a bad attitude executing it.

You are a well-oiled machine. But you also kind of feel like a machine. And what's weird is that you don't even like kombucha.

Stuck in the Lazy Way

If you're stuck in the Lazy Way, you do not cut up anything ahead of time . . . *ever*. You especially hate it when someone shares her styled stack of prepped lunches on Instagram. Who does she think she is?! And the voice in your head says, *She's better than me* obviously.

You always feel like you're behind, moving aside yesterday's breakfast dishes so you have space to cook dinner, but it's better than pretending to have it all together.

Right?

Pal, so, so wrong.

The Lazy Genius Way

If I haven't yet convinced you that the Lazy Genius Way is better, I'm doing a very poor job. Perhaps this list will convince you. If you're a Lazy Genius, you . . .

- experience a regular rhythm of preparedness in your kitchen.
- know what to prep ahead and what to leave for later.
- clean like a Lazy Genius, seeing it as a practice of getting ready for the next thing.
- rarely feel like you're drowning in your kitchen, and when you do, you know how to quickly find your breath again.

Let's go through our five steps because we are super good at them now.

1. **prioritize:** name what matters

2. **essentialize:** get rid of what's in the way

3. **organize:** put everything in its place

4. **personalize:** feel like yourself

5. **systemize:** stay in the flow

Step One
Prioritize
Your Prep

The Objective: Name what matters most.

Let's think about prep flow. You cycle through the same sort of flow for every single meal that comes out of your kitchen, even if each thought or task takes only two seconds. Not only that, multiple prep flows are happening at the same time. You clean up breakfast while getting lunch ready. You plan dinner while eating lunch. The prep flows will naturally overlap.

plan/shop

prepare
the space and
ingredients

clean
up   MEAL

gather to
eat it   cook
              the meal

Here's the rub. If you let too much time go between steps, you get a prep logjam. Accumulated dishes. No plans and no ingredients. You gather to eat dinner but around a table still covered in syrup from this morning's waffles.

Lazy Genius prep keeps you out of the logjam and in a flow. Let's figure out how.

Name
What
Matters

Your flow works best when you have what you need across the board, and luckily, you've already done a lot of that work.

When you prioritize, essentialize, organize, personalize, and systemize your space, your tools, the meals you cook, the plans you make, and the food you buy, prep is ready for action.

But you still must know what matters most about your prep, so let's think through that next.

What *Could* Matter About Your Prep?

Which of these fit you best?

- **Speed:** You want everything done quickly.
- **Cleanliness:** You want a dependable strategy to prevent or get rid of messes.
- **Teamwork:** You do *not* want to be the only one tapped into the prep flow.
- **Time of Day:** You must take certain hours off the table because of energy, a job, etc.
- **Predictability:** You want to know what's coming next without having to think about it.
- **Efficiency:** Different prep flows impact each other in a helpful way.
- **Simplicity:** You want the fewest number of steps to get the job done.

As always, add anything else that comes to mind.

What *Does* Matter About Your Prep?

It's time to start narrowing. What priorities stand out and which ones fade away? If you need help eliminating some options, imagine the entire prep flow and notice what feels important. Or do an actual prep flow for whatever meal you're in now and start paying attention.

What Matters *Most* About Your Prep?

Really, the question you're answering is what matters most about *how you live*, day in and day out in your kitchen. All the pieces connect together in this prep flow.

When you imagine yourself in your kitchen, what makes it most enjoyable to be there? How do you want to feel?

For me, I want the flow to feel calm but steady. I don't want the flow to stop.

If it's time to make lunch but I haven't cleaned up breakfast, if it's time to shop for groceries but I haven't made a plan, or if it's time to clean up dinner but the leftovers have already dried in the pan, I *do not like it.*

Basically, I'm in a constant state of asking the Magic Question (LGP #3) to keep the flow moving.

What can I do now to make prep easier later? *What can I do now to stay in the flow?*

That's why I rarely shop without a plan, gather without an intention, or go to bed with a dirty kitchen. It disrupts my prep flow, and keeping that flow going with that steady pulse matters most.

Do I sometimes whine when I forget there are dishes to wash and all I want to do is read my dystopian novel where a girl takes down the patriarchy? Yes, of course I do. But I also know that the ten minutes it will take to wash the dishes is ten minutes. If I wait until morning, it *feels* like thirty minutes. Then the flow is off, and I have a morning logjam.

Full disclosure: my husband cleans the kitchen pretty much every night. He knows it's a priority for me and loves me by making it his priority, too. Share the load if you can. Ask for help. Your family is a team.

Okay, you've prioritized, so now it's time to essentialize and get rid of those pesky logjam culprits.

Step Two Essentialize Your Prep

The Objective: Get rid of what's in the way.

Good news! You've already done so much of this. You've essentialized your planning, shopping, and cooking, and those choices will automatically have an effect on your prep flow.

However, those choices you made in the earlier chapters are expansive choices—what you'll eat all week for dinner, what tools you'll have in your kitchen for months and even years, what kinds of meals you'll make for this season of life.

Essentializing your prep is more specific.

You want to get rid of things that stop your flow in small, daily ways. Let's look at individual meals and tasks, and get specific.

Breakfast

- Your kids love scrambled eggs, but you usually say no. You think it's because you don't have time to cook the eggs, but really you don't have time to clean the pan because the nonstick coating is bad and the dried egg is super annoying to scrape off. Get rid of that pan.

- A favorite mug exponentially enhances your morning coffee experience, but the six mugs you don't care about are in the way. Get rid of those six mugs.
- The cereal is in the cabinet above the refrigerator because, as we already established, that's where your mom put it when you were growing up, but your own kids can't reach it. Put the cereal somewhere else.

Lunch

- You spend a lot of time researching creative lunches for your kids, but they are seriously fine with the same thing over and over. Get rid of creative prep.
- The lunch container you take to work looks pretty but is hard to clean, especially when it sits for six hours before you get home. Get rid of that lunch container.
- You have zero desire to prep your own bento-style lunches, but your ham sandwich feels like a failure of adulthood. Get rid of that expectation.

Dinner

- Your kids need hands-on help with homework, but you try to make dinner while they're asking you about common denominators. Prep dinner at a different time.
- You know that washing the pots and pans from dinner before the food dries on them will make your life better, but the breakfast and lunch dishes are stacked in the sink. Get rid of the habit of putting dirty dishes directly in the sink so you can easily run the soapy water when you need it.
- Everything you make for dinner gets put in separate bowls to take to the table, but then you're left with a mountain of dishes you do *not* want to wash. Get rid of table service and stick with pan-to-plate.

Snacks

- Kids are always asking if something is okay to eat, and you are out of decision-making energy by snack time. Get rid of the question by creating a kid-level bin of approved snacks.

- You're constantly throwing out slimy bell pepper slices you prepare as an afternoon snack. Get rid of bell peppers as a snack food.
- Your kids wander around the house with their snack cups and crumb-filled plates, and you don't know those dishes are out there until the dishwasher is humming. Get rid of missing dishes by doing a sweep of the house as part of your family clean-up routine.

Cleaning Up

- You think that a real cook has everything measured out ahead of time in tiny prep bowls, but then you're left having to wash tiny prep bowls. Get rid of the tiny prep bowls. Just pile everything on the cutting board instead.
- You're always moving mail from your Dirty Dishes Zone (an integral part of a Lazy Genius prep flow, detailed in the next section). Get rid of the tendency to put mail there by creating a different place it can easily go.
- A mess is stacked up at the end of the day, and you want to cry at having to deal with all those dishes right now. Get rid of procrastination and tend to the dishes after every meal.

Leftovers

- You keep purposely making extra because you think that's what people do, but no one in your house likes leftovers. Get rid of making leftovers on purpose.
- You grill extra chicken or roast a bigger pork shoulder, but the leftovers die before you figure out a way to use them. Get rid of winging it.
- Your plastic storage containers are old and have barely functioning lids, but you've been using them so long you don't even notice how frustrating they are. Get rid of broken, lidless, nonfunctional containers.

These are just ideas to get yours moving. Get rid of what's in the way so you can stay plugged into an enjoyable prep flow that works. Now we organize.

Step Three
Organize
Your Prep

The Objective: Put everything in its place.

Ready-made food in see-through containers is not what it means to organize your prep. What you really need is a way to organize your daily life in the kitchen so that your prep flow keeps moving, and we're going to do that with zones.

Organizing by Zone

Zones will change your life in the kitchen. I do not lie. Relegating a specific task to a certain area makes it so easy to decide what happens where.

I want to share three magical zones that will keep your prep flow from turning into a logjam. Add more, use one, do whatever you need, but these three are proven winners.

The Dirty Dishes Zone

Part of the prep flow logjam is the cleaning up of dirty dishes. Random bowls and cups from the many meals and snacks our people eat are spread out all over the place, and we think we have to clean up the dishes *fully* for it to count. Not true.

The Dirty Dishes Zone is a singular place on your counter specifically and *exclusively* for dirty dishes until you're ready to clean them. And the zone doesn't have to be huge. A one-foot-square area is awesome, but that zone is *only* for dirty dishes. Don't put other stuff there.

If you move all the dirty dishes to the Dirty Dishes Zone and do nothing else, it changes your space *and* positively impacts your flow. It's kind of wild. The other surfaces are clear, which is visually calming.

Plus, since they're in one place, you can more easily wash those dirty dishes or load them in the dishwasher in a single batch all at once whenever you're ready. It sounds simple, and it is. But it also creates a fantastic rhythm for you and your space.

The Eat This Zone

This zone is in your refrigerator. (You could have one in your freezer, too, if you're a freezer meal person.)

Designate one zone in your fridge—a shelf, a drawer, a plastic bin you add yourself—for Eat This food items. Prepped snacks, leftover dinner, wilted vegetables that need to find a life before they die, etc.

If you live in a house with ravenous children, you could even have a

Don't Eat This Zone so that your teenager doesn't eat all the cheese you need for tomorrow's pizza.

The act is simply that of moving a food from one place to another, from a crisper drawer to the zone, from a fridge shelf to the zone, from anywhere to the zone. Then you know where to look first when it's time to snack, prep dinner, or clean out the fridge.

By having a zone for those foods, your flow doesn't get clogged.

The What Are We Eating? Zone

Create a designated space where you write down what you'll be eating soon.

Why? If you have kids, you know why because you get asked "What's for dinner?" before breakfast is even a thought. But even beyond kids, knowing what's coming keeps your prep flow in motion.

Where you put your zone is up to you, but I recommend it be visible and not digital. Put a little whiteboard on your fridge or have a notepad that stays on the counter. Just make it easy to write on and easy to see.

What you write doesn't have to be long, detailed, or even chronological. If you know you want to make a Bolognese sauce at some point during the week because you have the ingredients and the craving, write that down so you'll remember, and don't write anything else. Be as detailed or as sparse as you like—whatever serves you.

Organizing by Task

You want to organize your *time* around tasks that matter most to your life in the kitchen. If you just wait around for things to take care of themselves or assume you'll get to it later, you'll almost definitely hit that logjam.

If you need some help Lazy Geniusing some of your tasks, you'll love Part 3. We Lazy Genius all kinds of things, but here are some specific tasks to consider if you want immediate help:

How to Prep Food (page 180)
How to Plan Freezer Meals (page 179)
How to Plan Breakfast (page 175)
How to Plan Lunch (page 176)
How to Clean the Kitchen (page 181)
Easy Tasks for Your Kids to Do in the Kitchen (page 184)
How to Plan a Month of Meals at Once (page 178)

Choose what you need based on what matters to you.

Now that your flow is moving, let's make sure you feel like yourself while you're in it.

Step Four
Personalize Your Prep

The Objective: Feel like yourself.

You do not have to be highly organized, highly skilled, or highly motivated to have a prep flow that changes your life. Do not be tricked by the voice in your head saying that you don't have what it takes to do this.

You do. Because you get to decide what you need.

This isn't about copying my way just because it works for me. That's likely a giant waste of your time.

Remember, your **personality, people, priorities, proficiency, process, pleasure, and peace** all play a role and are likely very different from mine or anyone else's. You and I cannot use the same system and expect it to work . . . because *we are not the same person.*

Claim what you love and need. Involve your people based on what *they* love and need. Make tiny decisions that help you feel above the fray and good about yourself, even if they seem silly to someone else.

I buy yummy-smelling dish soap even if it's more expensive because it makes me happy, and when I'm happy, I feel like myself.

No choice is too small.

Now let's talk about how to stay in the flow with your prep. Which is its own flow. We're flowing the flow!

Step Five
Systemize Your Prep

The Objective: Stay in the flow.

Seriously, systemizing your prep is the lifeblood of everything. When you keep that prep flow moving and those separate meal-prep flows from converging into something bigger than you can handle, you will absolutely enjoy being in your kitchen.

Rhythm happens by sticking with principles, not rules.

Principal Picks for Your Prep

Ask the Magic Question (LGP #3)

I have an entire list of ways to answer the Magic Question on page 183. Sometimes we need a quick reminder of even obvious things.

The point is to keep asking. What can you do now to make life easier later? What can keep the flow going in your kitchen? You can ignore everything else in this book *except that question* and still experience a marked difference. It is indeed magic.

Build the Right Routine (LGP #5)

Routines are not fifteen steps you do every single day and if you miss one, you fail. *No.* The right routine starts with what matters *and* with naming where you're going.

If your destination is a moving prep flow, think about what *you in your own kitchen with your own personality* can do to get there, *one small step at a time.*

Maybe you put all the breakfast dishes in the Dirty Dishes Zone before you start making school lunch. Maybe you put food you're done with in the Fridge Zone (page 181) while you keep making dinner; you're not putting it away, just *out of the way.*

It's writing down what you need to buy the minute you run out of something. It's letting the dirty water out of the sink right after the dishes are clean and not the next morning. It's all the little things that are easy to ignore but can quickly stop your flow.

Start Small

Speaking of little things, do not try to re-flow your kitchen all at once. I forbid it.

I've said this an excessive number of times, but I shall say it yet again: starting small means you actually do whatever it is you're trying to do. If you build it too big, nothing happens and you stay stuck. You know this, I know this, we all know this.

It is worth it to start small with one choice, one answer to the Magic Question, one meal, one expectation. Start small, and your system will build itself.

Set House Rules (LGP #6)

I heavily depend on House Rules to keep my prep flow moving, so in case my list inspires yours, here you go:

- Don't go to bed with a dirty kitchen.
- The person who empties a pan rinses it right away.
- Start the next meal only after the previous meal has been zoned.

No lie, when I started writing down my House Rules, I thought I had more. These three pack such a punch that they feel like ten rules in my head. That was kind of an exciting discovery, actually. I have only three House Rules for my prep, and I love them so much.

Keep naming what you love so much, too, and use principles to get there.

Remember the Path

First, *prioritize*: Name what matters about your prep flow, about the steady heartbeat of your kitchen. Name how you want to feel when you're in your hardest-working room.

Second, *essentialize*: Get rid of anything that gets in the way of that prep flow—tools that don't work, timings that don't support your life, expectations that don't make sense.

Third, *organize*: Remember that your prep flow adores zones. Start small with one zone (I recommend the Dirty Dishes Zone because we all have those), and then begin to structure your time and movement around those zones.

Fourth, *personalize*: Do whatever makes you feel like yourself as you move from meal to meal, task to task, day to day in your kitchen. Copying someone else's way is not the move. Do what *you want*.

Fifth, *systemize*: Use Lazy Genius principles to keep you moving without hemming you into a complicated system. If you're too excited about all the principles but know you need to start with one, start with the Magic Question. The answers will change your life one tiny answer at a time. After that, pick a House Rule, and watch your prep flow pick up a bit.

I can already feel the magic happening in your kitchen, and I'm so stoked for you.

And now it's time to gather.

table

Experiencing your meals

This is why we do what we do. Deep down, the magic of food is directly connected to eating and sharing. That's why everyone wants a space that's "good for entertaining." We're built for community and connection, and the table is one of the best places for it.

But so much keeps us stuck, not just from inviting people over but also from enjoying our everyday table.

Stuck in the Genius Way

If you're stuck thinking like a Genius, you think every meal must be cloaked in lively, vulnerable conversation on a beautifully set table. No one complains about the food. No one argues about cleaning up. Everyone lingers because they love each other so much. Those boxes of conversation starters get you bonus points.

When it's time to open the doors to other people, the gathering feels like a classy beer commercial. Everyone is always impressed with your food, but even more so at how you are a perfect, effortless, casual host.

Stuck in the Lazy Way

When you're stuck in the Lazy Way, your kids are often finished eating dinner before you even sit down because of all the ketchups and milks there are to fetch. You're still in pajamas at dinner, candles are a fire hazard, big kids are on their phones, and you roll your eyes at those conversation starters even though a conversation with people you love sounds kind of nice.

You're terrified of having anyone over because of how life has thrown up all over your house, plus the only food you really know how to make is macaroni and cheese, and not the homemade kind. It feels too overwhelming and hopeless, so you keep eating standing up or in front of the TV and offer to go out for pizza whenever anyone wants to get together for a meal.

The Lazy Genius Way
It's simple: the table serves what matters most to you, no matter who is around it.

That's really it. I'm not going to tell you what a Lazy Genius table looks like because only you know, but that's the point of all this. *You* name what matters most so that you can enjoy your table when it's just you on the couch or you and twenty people celebrating Thanksgiving.

Time to pull out our five steps:

1. **prioritize:** name what matters
2. **essentialize:** get rid of what's in the way
3. **organize:** put everything in its place
4. **personalize:** feel like yourself
5. **systemize:** stay in the flow

Let's gather.

Step One
Prioritize Your Table

The Objective: Name what matters most.

First, let's define *table*. I mean, we know what a table is, but in the context of this discussion, a table is *where you eat*. It's the avatar for where you gather for meals in your home.

You can experience the *idea* of the table in plenty of places: the couch, a blanket outside, breakfast in bed, etc. In fact, it's possible to not own a table at all and experience this whole section fully.

Since gathering is an area with highly unreasonable expectations, it is super important to name what matters most so you can start putting your energy into that thing.

Obviously, there are different iterations of the table depending on the meal and who's eating. There's you eating lunch alone, all the way to hosting a dozen friends for a summer cookout. There's a chance that what matters most for your everyday table is a little different from what matters when you're having people over, but don't assume that's the case until you name it.

Let's do that now.

What *Could* Matter About Your Table?

These are some broad strokes. Gathering for a meal is such a personal thing, so don't be weirded out if your priority isn't on this list. Just let it get you thinking. Which of these feel comfortable to you?

- **Food:** You want everything to be absolutely delicious and memorable.
- **Conversation:** As long as everyone is talking and connecting, you're happy.
- **Comfort:** The food, the chairs, and the conversation are all meant to make people feel good.
- **Ease:** Whatever you make and whoever you're feeding don't cause you stress.
- **Vibe:** You want your time at the table to feel a certain way.
- **Teamwork/Connection:** You want everyone at the table to feel part of the same experience, including serving and cleaning up.

If narrowing it down to one thing in this way doesn't land as well with you (which could be the case since the table is the most intangible of all our sections), view the table through these three lenses:

- **Experience** is how the gathering feels.
- **Aesthetics** is how the gathering looks.
- **Logistics** is how the gathering works.

Maybe one of those specific categories matters more than another, or maybe those three buckets give you some language to sift through a longer list of what could matter. Are you an aesthetics person more than a logistics person? That's a hugely helpful thing to know as you gather people around your table.

Right now, anything goes. Then we narrow.

What *Does* Matter About Your Table?

Think about all the meals you experience around your table and ask what makes them the most memorable or enjoyable. Remember, you want to have what you need, so naming what made you enjoy a meal means you might want to have more of that thing.

What brings you joy? Eliminate what's secondary to that.

What Matters Most About Your Table?

What matters most about your table will beautifully dictate just about every decision you make around it.

If what matters most is conversation, you will relax around the food you choose and how things look. You will set House Rules for your family about phones or books at the table and be a genius about topics of conversation when you gather.

Knowing what matters tells you what to do next.

Now let's get rid of what's in the way.

Step Two
Essentialize
Your Table

The Objective: Get rid of what's in the way.

Now that you know what matters most, you can see what doesn't belong in your kitchen anymore. If it doesn't support what matters, pass it along to someone else.

And as I did in previous sections, let me remind you that it's not time to organize. We're just removing things for now.

The Actual Table

Is your table too big or too small? If your top priority is comfort followed by conversation, your uncomfortable chairs and long table likely won't serve you well for long. Obviously don't just trash your table and chairs; I'm not crazy. But decide that they eventually need to go once you have the means to replace them with a round table and comfy chairs.

Plates and Linens

If your top priority is being casual, maybe it's time to say goodbye to the fine china or at the very least the fancy hutch that holds it. If you want a casual place to gather, it'll be a challenge to experience that in a room full of traditionally fancy things.

The inverse of this is true, too. If what matters most is that meals, especially dinner, feel really special, maybe the multi-colored plastic plates aren't your best choice. If you want durability for younger kids but not the primary colors, look into plastic plates in neutral colors that fit what matters most to you.

Do you have a stack of tablecloths but don't know where they are or the last time you used them? I used to have such a stash that creased so badly because they never left the closet. My stash has now shrunk to two tablecloths that I honestly still don't know where they are . . . which isn't much better. If I've gone this long without using a tablecloth, and by this long I mean at least a decade, I can probably survive without it.

Borrowing is always an option if you need something you've essentialized.

The point? Don't keep what you don't need or use.

Music

Music is such an integral part of gathering around the table, for good and bad.

If your top priority is a lively table, playing sad, moody music is not a great call, even if the Spotify playlist is titled "Dinner Party." Play something else.

If the top priority is conversation, having the music too loud can stop it from happening. Turn it down.

If your top priority is togetherness, arguing over what music gets played at the table does not help. Decide once (LGP #1) what day of the week each person gets to choose the music.

Expectations

This is the biggie.

Your stress around your table is, without question, exclusively due to unreasonable expectations of how things are supposed to be. *Exclusively.*

You could tell me, "No, Kendra, for real I live in the tiniest apartment and don't even have a table to sit around!" The floor is great, my friend. I'm serious. You can have no money, no space, no *table*, and your fear of gathering is still rooted in unreasonable expectations of how things are supposed to be.

Remember:

- You do not have to cook the meal.
- You do not have to have a tablescape.
- You do not have to impress people with how kind and gracious and "host-y" you are.
- You do not have to light candles.
- You do not have to know clever conversation starters.
- You do not have to have a clean house.
- You do not have to have a dirty house to prove that you're real.
- You do not have to even have a table.

If your experience around your table is rooted in performance and other people's presumptions about what that experience should look like, you will either be stressed out by gatherings or avoid them altogether. *Don't let your insecurity rob you of the joy of the table.*

The sooner you believe your home is worthy and capable of inviting people to it (which it is in literally any state or stage), the sooner you can get to gathering in a way that supports what matters to you.

Now let's organize what gets you there.

Step Three
Organize
Your Table

The Objective: Put everything in its place.

We're not going to talk about place settings or linen storage. Google will come in handy for the first and Martha Stewart for the second. In a Lazy Genius kitchen, we prioritize something different: the vibe.

Organizing by Task—Setting a Vibe

You might not think you're a vibe person, but you are. Everything is a vibe. You just get to decide what it is.

A vibe is really just a feeling, and certain experiences feel different in our memories because of a vibe, either good or bad.

You could go to a restaurant that has the most delicious food ever, but what if the vibe is bad? If the servers are rude, if the decorations are too precious, if the menu is printed so small you can't see it, if the other diners do not smile at you when you walk by, *that's not a great vibe.*

Every gathering has a vibe, even the ones that are just you, eating PB&J scraps while you lean against the counter scrolling Instagram. Which I have done *many a time.*

The question is, Is that the vibe you want? If it is, fantastic. If it isn't, let's organize what you need to gather with your preferred vibe.

Vibe Supplies

A vibe is simply a manufactured feeling. You are trying to create an environment that makes someone feel a certain way—comfortable, welcome, excited, laid back, surprised, interested, at ease. It's your call, and you already made it. You already named what mattered most about your table, and I bet it's a feeling.

My absolute favorite part about gathering people around a table is creating that feeling, setting that vibe. I want you to have vibe supplies at the ready, so we're going to name them so you can put them in their place.

The Vibe for Just You

How do you want your meal to feel when it's just you?

You might live alone, eat lunch alone, or find yourself eating dinner alone several nights a week, maybe because a partner or roommate is regularly out of the house.

If you want to feel peaceful, your vibe supplies would be an unscented candle (don't compete with food smells) in a portable vessel (in case you need to eat in another room), dishes that don't make you crazy because they're broken or stained or covered in cartoon dogs, and a quiet place to eat (or a working set of headphones).

Name what you want your vibe to be when it's just you, and know where to find the vibe supplies to feel it.

The Vibe for the Family

If you have younger kids, the vibe might be just plain fun (and a little bit of survival thrown in). Maybe you play happy classical music, ring a dinner bell when it's time to eat, and play the same little question game during dinner. Done.

If you have teenagers, the vibe could be warmth and safety. You want there to be the option for conversation and connecting on the days when everyone is actually eating together, especially since that happens more infrequently as kids get older.

For that, your vibe might start before dinner is even ready. You play music that everyone likes, you spend time in the kitchen and invite a kid to hang out with you to do homework close by. You light candles and ask for help tasting something to see what it needs. You create a long runway of warmth and safety so that when you do sit down to dinner, the door is already open.

If it's just you and a partner, dinner might be your favorite time to connect. Maybe you don't have kids, they're already out of the house, or they're tiny enough to be in bed by 6:30 p.m. Your vibe might be intimate connection. You light candles, you cook grown-up food at a grown-up pace, you listen to music the kids always make you turn off, and you just enjoy the process of making dinner and carry that over to the table. You're gathering the whole time.

The Vibe for a Group

I once had dinner at someone's house where the vibe was most certainly to have fun. The host had a beverage cart ready to go (I think people who prioritize beverages are often the most fun), and there were tiny umbrellas to put in our tea and lemonade and dinner cocktails.

Tiny umbrellas.

That is such a great vibe supply if you're into having fun. But if you own tiny umbrellas but can't find them, you don't get to experience a fun tiny umbrella vibe.

Know what vibe you want, gather any supplies you might need for it, put them in a single place, and get them out when it's time to gather.

And let's hope that when that happens, you'll have what you need to feel like yourself. Let's do that next.

Step Four
Personalize
Your Table

The Objective: Feel like yourself.

The table is the most vulnerable place to be yourself *and therefore the most powerful.*

The best way to personalize your table is to be yourself when you're there.

Invite others to be themselves. Ask questions, tell jokes even if they're bad, sit in silence when necessary, exchange that look with your spouse when your kid tells a story from school that's so sweet and ridiculous and you are so tired but love this kid so much.

The table is my favorite place to love people well, and it's a favorite place for all of us to *feel* loved.

When that matters most, the door is wide open for how you personally can make it happen.

Consider your **personality**. You don't have to become loud if you're naturally quiet or quiet if you're naturally loud. Just be *you.*

Think about the **process** of a meal. Do you want to sit down with everyone right away? Then a way to personalize your table is to make sure you *can*. Know that your process of cooking a meal needs to be done once it's time to sit. No scurrying for you.

And **people**. That's the best part. Personalize your table by surrounding it with people. You can live alone but still invite people over. If you live alone, you can enjoy the table with a beloved show. That's a real thing I did while I was away writing this book! I ate dinner with "friends"! They were just on a TV screen.

Laughing, human connection, not hiding who you are . . . you as *a person* make your table better, even if you're the only person there.

Step Five Systemize Your Table

The Objective: Stay in the flow.

Gathering around a table is the most intangible but the most powerful component of life in the kitchen. In fact, the table *begins in the kitchen.*

That's where your rhythm starts: at the stove or the counter, preparing the food, creating a vibe, and setting an intention to gather and connect.

In order to systemize your table, to enjoy the rhythm it offers, pay attention to what matters most, be purposeful in setting your vibe, and use some Lazy Genius principles to make gathering around the table an enjoyable thing.

Principal Picks for Your Table

Let People In (LGP #8)

If you're waiting to have people over until your house is in better shape, you're a better cook, or those people become better friends, stop.

Stop waiting. If you wait for things to be perfect or ideal, you will always be waiting. Instead, let people in. Let them into your home, your everyday life, and your mess. You also don't have to have a mess in order to be real. Clean houses are welcoming, too.

Be Kind to Yourself (LGP #13)

You don't have to know everything. You don't have to have the most beautiful dishes and cloth napkins. You can forget the sauce or spill a drink or forget to light the candles.

The kinder you are to yourself, especially in front of the people in your life, whether friend or family, the more you model kindness to them.

Start Small (LGP #2)

You might desperately desire to focus on the table and to gather people around it, but you've never done it before and you're afraid.

If you'd like to host Thanksgiving Dinner this year for your family of twenty, start with inviting a couple of friends over for dinner next week. Have over one family member, and then two. Start small in the number of people you have around your table and work your way up.

Of course, you can fill your home with thirty people without ever having had one person over, but I imagine feeding that many people would be a more pleasant experience if you start small first.

Decide Once (LGP #1)

Go ahead and decide now what you'll cook when new people come for dinner.

Every time someone is new, you make pizza or tacos or that chicken dish your mom taught you. Take away the stress of choosing so you can focus on being welcoming and creating a vibe to make the gathering feel the way you want it to feel.

Don't avoid the table because you don't feel like yourself there. Being yourself makes the table better, and you get to invite others to do the same.

Remember the Path

First, *prioritize*. Name what matters about gathering with your people to eat. Most likely it's a feeling, and putting a name to that feeling offers so much direction.

Second, *essentialize*. Get rid of whatever is in the way of that feeling. The clutter, the expectations, the china, the crumbs. Essentialize based only on what matters, not on what other people tell you should matter.

Third, *organize*. Remember that creating a vibe is simply a manufactured feeling, so name what contributes to your vibe, and have those vibe supplies in a place you can easily get to.

Fourth, *personalize*. Be yourself at the table, and invite everyone around it to do the same.

Fifth, *systemize*. The rhythm around the table begins in the kitchen, and as you use Lazy Genius principles to experience that rhythm, you'll enjoy not only your time around the table more but the person you bring to it as well.

Pal, that was a lot. You just worked super hard.

How are you feeling? Are you excited? Feel peaceful and limber like we just left yoga class?

(The regular kind, not the hot kind. If you've read *The Lazy Genius Way*, you already know I tried that, and *it wasn't great*.)

Now that you've read Parts 1 and 2, here's what we're going to do next.

The Deal with Part 3

Part 3 is the best encyclopedia for being a person in the kitchen, ever. It is a beautiful, helpful, rad collection of all kinds of specific skills and resources so you can learn to **use what you have**.

You can read straight through, or at the very least skim, but know that everything in Part 3 is specifically labeled, efficiently short, and exceedingly helpful.

Here we go.

Use What You Have

TO DO

You will never learn everything. How's that for an introduction? But you just won't. It's better to know that now and accept it so you can move on to what matters.

However, it is nice to have a trusted voice tell you some stuff you might not know but would like to, especially if, again, you're thirty-seven and know how to use hyaluronic acid but do *not* know how to use tongs.

This is a safe space, and all these resources are meant to help you with what you don't yet know.

If you don't want to know something, skip it. If you do, this is why we love page numbers.

I hope this section is a go-to reference for you for years to come.

TECHNIQUES
How to Cook

- How to Cook Chicken (page 143), including a recipe for Change Your Life Chicken (page 144)
- How to Make Soup (page 145)
- How to Make Salad (page 146)
- How to Roast Stuff (page 147)
- How to Grill Stuff (page 150)
- How to Make a Marinade (page 151)

TASTE
How to Make Food Taste Good

- How to Tell If a Recipe Is Any Good (page 153)
- 27 Ingredient Combinations That Will Never Let You Down (page 154)
- 22 Ingredients That Pack a Flavor Punch (page 155)
- Staple Ingredients for Nine Different Cuisines (page 156)
- The Liquid Index Ingredient Guide (page 158)
- How to Add Freshness to Repetitive Meals (page 160)

TOOLS
How to Use Your Stuff

- Tools for Roasting (page 161)
- Tools for Baking (page 162)
- Tools for Grilling (page 163)
- Tools for Sautéing (page 164)
- Tools for Steaming (page 164)
- Tools for Braising, Soups, and Stews (page 165)
- Tools for Cooking Pasta, Rice, and Grains (page 165)
- How to Use Your Instant Pot (page 166)
- Tools for Cutting and Blending Food (page 167), including my TED talk on wooden cutting boards (page 168)
- Lazy Genius Knife Skills (page 169)
- Tools for Moving Food Around and How to Do It (page 170)
- Tools for Measuring (page 173)

TASKS
How to Keep Up with It All

- How to Plan Breakfast (page 175)
- How to Plan Lunch (page 176)
- When You Don't Have a Plan (page 177)
- How to Plan a Month of Meals at Once (page 178)
- How to Plan Freezer Meals (page 179)
- How to Prep Food (page 180)
- How to Clean the Kitchen (page 181)
- How to Clean out the Fridge (page 182)
- 28 Ready-to-Go Answers to the Magic Question (page 183)

TIPS
How to Make Hard Stuff Easier

- Easy Tasks for Your Kids to Do in the Kitchen (page 184)
- How to Never Run Out of Food at a Party (page 185)
- How to Choose What Food to Serve at a Party (page 186)
- How to Feed a Crowd (page 187)
- How to Host Thanksgiving (page 189), including a recipe for Lazy Genius Thanksgiving Turkey (page 190)

TECHNIQUES
How to Cook

How to Cook Chicken

	breast with skin + bone	thigh with skin + bone	boneless skinless breast	boneless skinless thigh	legs	tenderloin	ground chicken	whole chicken
sauté	Don't do it!	Don't do it!	Go for it!	Go for it!	Don't do it!	Go for it!	Go for it!	Don't do it!
grill		Go for it!	Go for it!	Go for it!	Go for it!	Go for it!	Don't do it!	Don't do it!
roast	Go for it!	Go for it!	Don't do it!		Go for it!	Don't do it!	Don't do it!	Go for it!
fry			Go for it!	Go for it!		Go for it!	Don't do it!	Don't do it!
poach	Don't do it!	Don't do it!	Go for it!	Go for it!	Don't do it!	Go for it!	Don't do it!	Don't do it!
braise	Go for it!	Go for it!	Don't do it!		Go for it!	Don't do it!	Don't do it!	Don't do it!

Not every cut of chicken works for every method, so use this table to know the best way to cook whatever kind you bought at the store.

P.S.: If you don't already eat chicken thighs, you should start. Not only are they more flavorful and juicy than chicken breasts, they are more affordable.

How to Make Change Your Life Chicken

This meal will change your life because it stands on its own, there's zero cleanup, you can use whatever ingredients you have, it's foolproof, and it's absolutely delicious.

OPTIONS: Vary the flavors and ingredients.
- Toss the vegetables with a spice blend.
- Use different vegetables or vegetable combos each time.
- Rub the chicken with grated lemon zest and chopped rosemary.

The method always works as long as you have bone-in, skin-on chicken thighs. If there is no bone or skin, it's not Change Your Life Chicken.

What You Need
- chicken thighs with bone and skin (1 to 2 per adult)
- 1 to 2 cups of chopped vegetables per person (such as onion, carrot, potato, green bean, asparagus, leek, sweet potato, cauliflower)
- vegetable/canola oil
- salt and pepper

How You Make It
1. **Preheat the oven to 500°F.** Not a typo. Five hundred degrees.
2. **Line a sheet pan with heavy-duty foil and then with parchment paper.** The pan needs to be big enough to hold your vegetables comfortably—not too close together, not too far apart. The foil keeps the pan clean; the parchment paper keeps the food from sticking. Or just use nonstick foil if you want.
3. **Toss your chopped vegetables with just enough oil to give them a sheen, more salt than you think you need, and some black pepper.** Consider the cooking times for the vegetables you choose; the longer they will need to cook, the smaller you'll need to cut them. Spread the veggies on the baking sheet.
4. **Peel the skin back from (but not off) the chicken, then season and pat dry with paper towels.** Don't wig out. This is how you get magic crusty chicken skin. The best method is to place the chicken skin side down, season the undersides, flip, pull back the skin, season the top, put the skin back, and pat dry. Why? The chicken needs to be salted on both sides, but you want to salt it *under* the skin. Going in this order ensures you don't dry the skin and then realize you forgot to season the undersides.
5. **Place the chicken skin side up directly on top of the vegetables.** Here's what happens: the fat from the chicken skin will seep down onto the vegetables underneath the chicken, imparting flavor and moisture, while the exposed vegetables get a tiny bit of char.
6. **Bake at 500°F for 50 minutes.** Don't worry if the chicken will be done; it will be. And we don't have to be concerned about the vegetables burning at such a high temperature because they're nestled closely together. The most you'll get will be a few crusty edges, and those are delightful.

Rule #1: Season every layer.

Salt does more than make things taste salty. In proper amounts, it increases sweetness and reduces bitterness. It is important for flavor and for drawing out moisture. Your soup will lack flavor if you simply add salt to the pot at the end.

Rule #2: Soup needs contrast.

Serve crunchy croutons on top of a smooth soup. Cook vegetables to varying degrees of tenderness so everything doesn't just turn to mush. Top hearty bowls of soup with something fresh or bright, like fresh herbs or a squeeze of citrus. Top spicy bowls of soup with something cooling, like sour cream, cheese, or avocado. Top mild bowls of soup with something spicy, like chili sauce or pickled jalapeño.

Rule #3: Go in the right order.

1. **Brown the meat:** If you're using it, especially red meat. Remove.
2. **Sauté the aromatics in some kind of fat**: Chopped onion, carrot, celery, leek, bell pepper, garlic, ginger, and chili pepper are great aromatics. Oil, butter, ghee, or rendered fat from the meat are great choices for sautéing the vegetables.
3. **Quick sauté any other vegetables**: Chopped or sliced asparagus, mushrooms, zucchini, eggplant, green beans, cabbage, etc. Throw in a pat of butter or glug of oil if the pan is dry.
4. **Add liquid**: Chicken stock, beef stock, vegetable stock, coconut milk, crushed tomatoes, or, of course, water—although you don't get any flavor with water.
5. **Bring to a simmer.** A simmer is tiny chill bubbles, not big excited ones.
6. **Add heavies**: Meat (including raw chicken that will gently cook in the soup), beans, chopped potatoes, pasta, grains.
7. **Simmer until everything is tender and happy**.
8. **Taste**. If it doesn't sing, try adding salt to make everything pop. If it feels like the flavors are too far apart, add an acid, like lemon juice or red wine vinegar. If it tastes good but is boring, add a flavorful topping.

How to Make Salad

Rule #1: Make and toss your salad in a *big* bowl.

Cramming everything into a small bowl, pouring dressing over it, and trying to fork-toss it without everything falling out is why we hate making salads. Use tongs and a big bowl to gently toss everything together.

Rule #2: Salads need contrast.

The best salads have contrasting textures, temperatures, flavors, and even colors. Standard house salads have all cold crunchy things—iceberg lettuce, cherry tomatoes, cucumbers, and dressing. But if you add crunchy bacon, some creamy gorgonzola cheese, grilled chicken, and toasted nuts, you add contrast and therefore have a much better salad.

There are two different kinds of **crunchy**: *crisp* crunchy, like raw vegetables, and *crunchy* crunchy, like nuts and croutons. Sometimes you need both kinds of crunchy, but every salad needs at least one type.

Now you want to contrast that crunchiness with **creaminess.** You can get that with more than just ranch dressing. Cheese, beans, and even roasted sweet potatoes are great sources.

Next is **volume**. Not math volume but flavor volume. Some foods are quiet and others are loud. Bibb lettuce is quiet. Radicchio is loud. If you have a salad of all quiet things, it'll be a boring salad.

Temperature contrast is often ignored. Warm components make salads very happy. Think grilled steak, hot bacon dressing, or croutons fresh from the pan.

A Master List of Salad Ingredients

Because sometimes you don't know something could go into a salad until someone tells you.

- ☐ roasted vegetables
- ☐ chickpeas
- ☐ black beans
- ☐ quinoa
- ☐ rice
- ☐ grilled vegetables
- ☐ caramelized onions

- ☐ grilled chicken
- ☐ steak
- ☐ salmon
- ☐ hard-boiled eggs
- ☐ fried egg
- ☐ bacon
- ☐ cheddar
- ☐ blue cheese
- ☐ feta

- ☐ queso fresco
- ☐ goat cheese
- ☐ fresh mozzarella
- ☐ shaved Parmesan
- ☐ sunflower seeds
- ☐ pumpkin seeds
- ☐ sesame seeds
- ☐ pecans
- ☐ walnuts

- ☐ peanuts
- ☐ croutons
- ☐ dried cranberries
- ☐ fresh blueberries
- ☐ diced apples
- ☐ clementine wedges
- ☐ pears
- ☐ avocado

- ☐ cucumber
- ☐ onion
- ☐ tomato
- ☐ all the greens
- ☐ pickled onions
- ☐ pickled jalapeños
- ☐ fresh herbs

Here are four basic tenets of roasting . . .

#1: Fat + Salt

Roasting is not a nonfat ordeal. Without fat, the food is likely to burn rather than cook, the texture won't be right, and it doesn't taste as good.

Salt makes your food taste like the best version of itself. It also draws moisture from the food, which is important in getting that crisp texture you want from roasting. There's a chance you're not salting your food enough, so try using more than you normally do and see what happens. In case you're curious, I prefer kosher salt.

#2: Foil + Parchment

This is a Lazy Genius tenet of roasting, not a universal one. However, lining your pan creates the easiest cleanup on the planet. I realize it also might not be great for the planet if you're in a no-waste house. I admire that and will not make anyone feel guilty about living either way.

You can use nonstick foil by itself, but I personally have not had great experiences with its doing its job. I use heavy-duty foil to protect the pan and conduct heat, and I use parchment paper to prevent the food from sticking.

#3: High Heat

If your oven is set lower than 400°F, you're not roasting, you're baking. You need a higher temperature to get the crispy, caramelized edges that make roasting magical.

#4: Space

The more space around your food, the more crispy and golden brown it will be.

If you are roasting multiple ingredients on one sheet pan (which is a great strategy), name what you want for each particular ingredient. For example, if you want very crispy potatoes but barely crispy green beans, spread the potatoes farther apart on one half of the pan and the green beans closer together on the other half. It all depends on what *you* want out of the final product.

How to Roast Stuff

Roasting is cooking food with hot indirect heat (like in an oven) and often in a single layer. The food darkens in color and is often crunchy on the outside and tender on the inside.

Why do it? Because it's stupid-easy, there's no cleanup, and it has great flavor.

How to Roast Stuff

TYPE	TEMP	TIME	TIPS
Asparagus	up to 425°F	15–25 min.	thinner stalks get less time
Beans—canned or already cooked	up to 450°F	10–30 min.	mix with other foods/liquids so they don't burn
Broccoli—florets and chopped stems	up to 500°F	15–25 min.	a quick steam beforehand or roasting straight from frozen improves final texture
Cabbage— cut into slabs	up to 450°F	15–25 min.	season well—thick slices won't caramelize the same
Carrots—small whole, sliced, diced	up to 500°F	20–50 min.	smaller pieces get less time— whole need lots of room
Cauliflower—florets and chopped stems	up to 500°F	20–35 min.	More water content than broccoli, so it stays more tender during roasting
Corn— on or off the cob	up to 450°F	15–25 min.	off cob burns quickly because of all the natural sugars—wrap cobs in foil and roast 20–25 minutes
Green beans—fresh	up to 500°F	15–30 min.	very forgiving and delicious a little charred
Mushrooms— whole, halved	up to 450°F	20 min.	give lots of room and more oil than you think you need
Onion—sliced, wedged, diced	up to 500°F	20–50 min.	soft when nestled; charred when spread out
Peppers— sliced, cubed	up to 500°F	10–45 min.	fajita-style slices cook quickly, bigger chunks are forgiving due to high water content
Potatoes—sweet and white, all sizes	up to 500°F	25–50 min.	the bigger the piece, the more time it needs— salt more than you think
Summer squash & zucchini— halved or sliced	up to 450°F	15–30 min.	roast flesh side down for best color and flavor
Tomatoes— cherry, wedged, canned	up to 450°F	10–30 min.	versatile, delicious when charred, great bed for eggs
Chicken—bone-in, skin-on breasts	425°F	35–45 min.	dry skin = crispy skin— season more than you think
Chicken—bone-in, skin-on thighs	475°F	40–50 min.	dry skin = crispy skin— season more than you think

TYPE	TEMP	TIME	TIPS
Chicken—drumsticks	400°F	30 min.	dry skin = crispy skin—season more than you think
Chicken—boneless, skinless	400°F	20 min.	season/marinate at least 20 minutes ahead of time
Pork—boneless chops, about 1 inch thick	400°F	30–40 min.	season/marinate at least 20 minutes ahead of time
Pork—whole tenderloin	400–450°F	20–25 min.	start in preheated sheet pan to sear—flip midway
Sausage—whole links	425°F	35–40 min.	put in direct contact with pan to get seared casing
Sausage—links sliced into 1-inch pieces	425°F	15–20 min.	cushion with other foods to keep moist
Steak—whole, about 1 inch thick	450°F	10–15 min.	in sheet pan, arrange vegs, grill rack, whole steak
Steak—in 1-inch slices	400°F	10–15 min.	put in direct contact with pan to get sear
Meatballs—size of golf ball	425°F	12–15 min.	if going from frozen, add 3–5 minutes
Salmon—skin-on fillets	425°F	12–15 min.	roast skin side down
Shrimp—with or without peel	400°F	6–8 min.	season or marinate really well, especially with peel on
Eggs—cracked whole into sheet pan	425°F	7–9 min.	in bed of already roasted vegetables or atop sauce

How to Grill Stuff

If you're comfortable cooking on your stovetop, you can cook on a grill.

Rule #1: Preheat the grill.
If you put food on a cold grill, it will absolutely stick and will not taste grilled.

Rule #2: Clean the grill while it's preheating.
Don't worry about cleaning your grill after you finish using it. All the food will cook off when you're preheating it the next time. Just scrub it after it's preheated and before you oil it.

Rule #3: Oil the grill.
If you don't oil the grill, your food will stick. Pour vegetable oil into a small bowl, soak it up with a small wad of paper towels, and use tongs to swipe the oil along the grates. Don't do this until you're ready to cook.

Rule #4: Leave the food alone.
The longer you leave it on the grill, the more flavor will develop and the easier it will be to flip. The only exception is sugary stuff, like barbecued chicken. In that cause, choose lower heat and flip often.

Rule #5: Close the lid.
When do you close the lid? Pretty much always. A closed lid doesn't mean the food will steam; it means it will have consistent heat. Because of physics I don't understand, opening the lid on a gas grill cools it down and on a charcoal grill it heats it up. Keep your lid closed as much as possible.

Rule #6: If your food tastes like fire, you probably haven't salted it enough.
That's it. That's the rule.

Rule #7: Google how long to cook something specific.
It's okay if you don't intuitively know, even for vegetables. Ask the internet your specific questions for how long something should cook. If you're worried about underdone meat, get yourself an instant-read thermometer and never worry again.

Why? To get flavor into the meat and create tenderness.

What's most important? Salt, fat, and acid. Aromatics and herbs are optional but lovely.

How long can it marinate? Chicken, 2 days; beef and pork, up to 5 days, as long as the meat itself is still fresh within that window.

How to use it? Make sure it's coating every bit of the meat.

When to pull the marinated meat out of the fridge? About 30–45 minutes before cooking.

Can I dump the bag of meat and marinade into a pan? No, the excess liquid will prevent your meat from browning. Remove the meat from the marinade with tongs or something slotted. Discard any leftover marinade that's been in contact with the meat.

How to Make a Marinade

Choose Your Own Adventure

	FAT	ACID	SALT	EXTRAS
Citrus Herb	olive oil, grapeseed oil	lemon juice, orange juice, lime juice	salt	garlic, fresh parsley, basil, thyme, rosemary, crushed red pepper flakes
East Asian	peanut oil, sesame oil, ghee	rice wine vinegar, ponzu, lemon juice	salt, soy sauce, miso	chili paste, ginger, garlic, cilantro, mirin, Chinese five-spice powder
Tex-Mex	olive oil, grapeseed oil, canola oil	lime juice, apple cider vinegar	salt	chili powder, cumin, coriander, jalapeño, cilantro, honey
Mediterranean	olive oil, grapeseed oil	balsamic vinegar, red wine vinegar, lemon juice	salt, capers, anchovies	fresh basil, parsley, and mint; garlic

TASTE
How to Make Food Taste Good

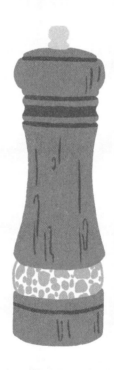

Do the ingredients go together?

Some combos you already trust: tomato and basil, chicken and rosemary, broccoli and cheese. Some sound suspect.

If you're unsure, use Google. Search the ingredients in question with plus signs to make sure you get results that include all of it—for example, chicken+potatoes+raisins. If you see a lot of recipe options, you know it's a combo that's been tested, even if you've never seen it before. If you do not see a lot of recipe options or the ones you see don't sound great, skip that recipe and try something else. *There are plenty of recipes out there.*

How does the recipe use salt?

If you combine the best foods in the world but don't add salt, the food will not shine. Salt is essential, so pay attention to how the recipe uses it.

If you're reading a soup recipe, and the only time you add salt is at the end "to taste," run for the hills. I want you listening to recipe developers who value salt in a way that makes your meals fantastic, not mediocre.

If a recipe contains less than ½ teaspoon of salt for the entire thing, it will not taste good. I have never made a meal that used so little and tasted as good as it could.

If a recipe encourages you to salt every layer and taste as you go, stay put.

How does the recipe utilize heat for flavor?

When food comes in contact with direct, powerful heat, flavor gets its wings. Think about the difference between a piece of grilled chicken and a piece that's boiled in water. One makes you happy and the other you feed to the cat.

This is why many slow-cooker recipes aren't amazing. The lack of direct heat (sautéing/grilling) or high indirect heat (a hot oven for roasting) doesn't give you the best flavor.

Notice if any ingredients come in contact with a pan or get hit with a temperature that's higher than 400°F. If so, you're in good shape. If not, see if you can adjust the recipe to allow heat to give more flavor—that is, sauté the vegetables or sear the meat beforehand.

27 Ingredient Combinations
That Will Never Let You Down

Use these in the Liquid Index (page 158), on pizza, for breakfast, whatever you want. Just know that putting these flavors together *always* works.

- tomato, basil, and mozzarella cheese
- spicy sausage, sweet potato, and greens
- lemon, olive oil, any herb
- artichokes, spinach, garlic, Parmesan cheese, and cream
- butternut squash, spinach, and bacon
- beef, garlic, and ginger
- beef, mushrooms, and red wine
- steak, potatoes, and horseradish
- Brussels sprouts, bacon, and onion or garlic
- chicken, potatoes, Dijon mustard, and thyme
- chicken, potatoes, garlic, and rosemary
- chickpeas, cumin, and cilantro
- shrimp, corn, and cilantro
- eggplant, mozzarella cheese, and basil

- eggs, bacon, cheese, and spinach
- firm white fish, tomato, and onion
- bacon, leeks, and cream
- mushrooms, shallots, and garlic
- pasta, garlic, and Parmesan cheese
- pasta, tomato, garlic, and basil
- peas, bacon, and cream
- pork, onions, garlic, and ginger
- potatoes, bacon, and cheese
- shrimp, garlic, and lime
- butternut squash, butter, red pepper flakes, and salt
- chorizo, sweet potatoes, and orange
- zucchini, tomato, basil, and garlic

22 Ingredients

That Pack a Flavor Punch

When you need some bang for your buck in a recipe, these ingredients explode.

- curry paste
- chili paste
- sun-dried tomatoes
- chipotles in adobo sauce
- honey
- capers
- herbs and spices of all kinds
- citrus, both zest and juice
- horseradish
- wasabi
- miso paste
- mustards
- toasted sesame oil
- olives and tapenade
- bacon and pancetta
- pickled vegetables
- saffron
- soy sauce
- fish sauce
- vinegars
- tamarind
- pesto

Staple Ingredients for Nine Different Cuisines

Countries are large, and their flavors are varied.
These ingredients are just a basic overview.

CHINESE

Aromatics
garlic
ginger
chili peppers
scallions

Herbs, Spices, Flavors
Chinese five-spice powder (usually cinnamon, peppercorns, clove, fennel seed, and star anise)
hoisin sauce
toasted sesame oil
soy sauce
rice wine vinegar

Other Ingredients
rice
vegetables, especially cabbage
tofu
duck
chicken
seafood

FRENCH

Aromatics
onion
shallot

Herbs, Spices, Flavors
tarragon
parsley
thyme
mustard
wine
flavorful stock

Other Ingredients
butter
cheese
cream
eggs
pastry
meat, including pork, beef, chicken, veal
seafood
potatoes

GREEK

Aromatics
garlic
bell peppers
onion

Herbs, Spices, Flavors
olive oil
oregano
mint
lemon
cinnamon
honey
thyme

Other Ingredients
lamb
fish
chicken
tomatoes
eggplant
cheese, especially feta
fennel
figs
spinach
zucchini
yogurt
phyllo dough
rice

INDIAN

Aromatics
ginger
garlic
chili peppers

Herbs, Spices, Flavors
cardamom
cumin
fenugreek
turmeric
coriander
cinnamon
cloves
curry powder
anise
nutmeg
tamarind
cilantro
mint
saffron

Other Ingredients
tomatoes
cauliflower
eggplant
peas
spinach
chicken
lentils
potatoes
coconut milk
ghee (clarified butter)

ITALIAN

Aromatics
garlic
bell peppers

Herbs, Spices, Flavors
anchovies
basil
oregano
capers
lemon
olive oil
thyme
balsamic vinegar
wine, especially
  Marsala

Other Ingredients
tomatoes
pasta
cheese
fish
sausage
chicken
veal
eggplant
fennel
artichokes
spinach
mushrooms
zucchini
olives

JAPANESE

Aromatics
ginger
chili peppers
scallion

Herbs, Spices, Flavors
soy sauce
yuzu
sesame oil and
  seeds
dashi
bonito
mirin
pickled vegetables
sake
wasabi

Other Ingredients
rice
seafood
noodles
steamed
  vegetables

MEXICAN

Aromatics
chili peppers
garlic
onion

Herbs, Spices, Flavors
cilantro
cumin
chili powder
lime, both juice
  and zest
orange, both juice
  and zest
saffron
oregano

Other Ingredients
beans
corn
tortillas
tomatoes
salsas
avocado
chicken
beef
pork
rice

MIDDLE EASTERN

Aromatics
garlic
ginger
onion

Herbs, Spices, Flavors
sumac
lemons, especially
  preserved lemons
dill
mint
oregano
coriander
cumin
cloves
nutmeg
oregano
ras el hanout,
  a spice blend
tahini
honey

Other Ingredients
yogurt
feta cheese
chicken
goat
lamb
eggplant
tomatoes
chickpeas
olives
pistachios
pomegranates
lentils
rice
walnuts

THAI

Aromatics
garlic
ginger
lemongrass
chili peppers
bell peppers

Herbs, Spices, Flavors
Thai basil
cilantro
mint
fish sauce
peanuts
curry powder
turmeric
coriander
cumin
lime, both zest
  and juice
coconut milk

Other Ingredients
noodles
rice
fish

The Liquid Index Ingredient Guide

So many options are at your fingertips, and here's
where you decide what to use.

START WITH . . .

Aromatics

onion (red, yellow, white)

shallots

scallions

leeks

carrots

celery

bell peppers (red, green,
yellow, orange)

chili peppers (jalapeño,
poblano, Thai, etc.)

lemongrass

fennel

garlic

ginger

Bite-Sized Protein

chicken (ground or cubed
boneless thighs, diced
boneless breast, diced
tenderloin)

pork (ground or cubed
tenderloin, cubed chops)

beef (ground or cubed
sirloin, cubed strip steak)

ground turkey

shrimp

sausage (pork, chicken,
turkey, chorizo)

firm white fish (cod, bass,
grouper)

beans (black, chickpeas,
cannellini, pinto, kidney)

Fat

olive oil

canola/vegetable oil

grapeseed oil

butter

ghee (clarified butter)

coconut oil

ADD BULK WITH . . .

beans (black, chickpeas,
cannellini, pinto, kidney)

potatoes (roasted or
steamed)

sweet potatoes (roasted
or steamed)

asparagus (roasted,
steamed, sautéed, or raw)

green beans (roasted
steamed, sautéed, or raw)

tofu

beets (roasted, steamed)

broccoli (roasted, steamed,
raw if small)

broccolini (roasted, steamed,
sautéed)

Brussels sprouts (roasted)

cabbage (green, savoy,
napa, red)

artichokes (canned and
drained)

cauliflower (roasted,
steamed, raw if small)

corn kernels

eggplant (roasted, steamed,
sautéed, or raw)

hearty greens (kale, bok
choy, chard)

spinach

winter squash (butternut or
acorn, roasted, steamed)

yellow squash and zucchini

okra (roasted or steamed)

green peas

snap peas

mushrooms (all kinds,
sautéed, roasted, raw)

tomatoes (fresh or canned,
diced or whole)

ADD LIQUID . . .

**(Some or a lot. If you don't
add any, congratulations,
your sauté is done.)**

stock or broth (chicken, beef,
vegetable)

wine (white, red, sake)

beer

coconut milk

cream

canned tomatoes

fruit or citrus juices

water

soy sauce

teriyaki sauce

Asian sauce or marinade

PUT IT IN . . .
omelet
fried rice
bread bowl
taco shells
tortillas
pita breads
lettuce cups/wraps
quesadillas
quiche or frittata
wonton or eggroll wrappers
hollowed-out bell peppers
roasted zucchini boats
salad (pasta, grain, or green)
lasagna

OR PUT IT ON . . .
grains (barley, bulgur,
    quinoa)
rice (white, brown, wild)
lentils
beans
couscous
Israeli couscous
pasta
grits
polenta
roasted or steamed
    cauliflower
roasted or mashed potatoes
roasted or mashed sweet
    potatoes
whole baked russet or sweet
    potatoes
pizza dough
flatbreads
naan
tortilla chips for nachos

ADD SOME TOPPINGS
nuts (toasted)
fresh herbs (basil, cilantro,
    parsley)
cheese (feta, blue, goat,
    mozzarella, Parmesan,
    queso fresco, cheddar)
tender greens (arugula,
    shredded lettuce, napa
    cabbage)
corn (fresh, sautéed,
    roasted)
avocado
diced or sliced cucumber
pickled vegetables (ginger,
    jalapeño, onions,
    cucumber)
radishes
pomegranate seeds
sour cream
yogurt
sauces and dressings

How to Add Freshness to Repetitive Meals

1. Add an herb.
It adds brightness, freshness, and flavor.

Add cilantro to chili, basil to pasta, green onions to stir-fries, parsley to roast chicken. Fold herbs into sauces and dressings, add them to salads, and blend them with oil and garlic for a sauce to drizzle over grilled or roasted meats.

2. Squeeze on some citrus.
Lemon, orange, lime, grapefruit, and all their iterations add acid for brightness and flavor. Acid not only cuts the salt and richness in foods but it also balances everything out with a beautiful sparkly flavor.

Squeeze lime juice onto roast pork, lemon onto roasted potatoes, and orange into an Asian marinade for pork.

3. Add a sauce.
Sauces transform ordinary ingredients into something special. A piece of grilled chicken can take on a million different personalities based on what sauce you choose.

Use stuff from a bottle—salad dressing, drizzle sauce, dips—or make your own from a trusted source. My favorite sauce whisperer is Bri McKoy, who has now been mentioned three times in this book. Go follow her on Instagram, please. She is a delight. @brimckoy

4. Make a switch.
If you always make stir-fries with carrots and broccoli, switch it up one night with carrots and mushrooms. Swap chicken for steak in tacos, or put different beans in your chili. Think about a way to make the same recipe with one or two differences to create a different meal.

5. Change the location.
Eating at the table over and over again, likely in the same chair, can feel grounded but also gets a little boring. Switch seats, move a table outside, eat in the driveway, or let your tiny kids eat dinner in a closet or blanket fort, or something random when you need a flash of freshness.

TOOLS
How to Use Your Stuff

- Tools for Roasting
- Tools for Baking
- Tools for Grilling
- Tools for Sautéing
- Tools for Steaming
- Tools for Braising, Soups, and Stews
- Tools for Cooking Pasta, Rice, and Grains
- How to Use Your Instant Pot
- Tools for Cutting and Blending Food (including my TED talk on wooden cutting boards)
- Lazy Genius Knife Skills
- Tools for Moving Food Around and How to Do It
- Tools for Measuring

TOOLS FOR ROASTING

ROASTING is cooking food with high but indirect heat, like in a 400°F or hotter oven. It's best for when you want foods with texture and crispiness, and for recipes that lend themselves to foods being cooked in one layer. Think roasted potatoes, chicken with crispy skin, and salmon that gets crispy on top but stays tender inside.

Recommended tools:

- **oven-safe skillet:** cast iron and stainless steel are best, copper and aluminum are the most finicky, and nonstick types are good only if made to be oven-safe
- **sheet pan:** like a cookie sheet, with low sides
- **roasting pan:** higher sides, like the kind you see a Thanksgiving turkey in
- **Dutch oven:** will work for roasting, but the high sides don't allow as much heat circulation, which means the skin might not get as crispy

TOOLS FOR BAKING

BAKING is cooking food with low but indirect heat, like in a less than 400°F oven. Think casseroles, lasagna, baked chicken and rice dishes, chicken pot pie, and obviously desserts. There are lots of options, but you don't need them all. Just pick what does the jobs you need done.

Recommended tools:

- **square/rectangular baking dishes** (ceramic, glass)
- **pie plates** (ceramic, glass)
- **disposable aluminum baking pans** (for when you want to share)
- **sheet pans/cookie sheets**
- **muffin tins/loaf pans**
- **variable,** anything that is a *conductor* of heat (like glass, ceramic, and aluminum)

If you want bread-baking tools, the best resource out there is Bonnie Ohara of "Alchemy Bread" (@alchemybread). Let her be your bread-baking guru.

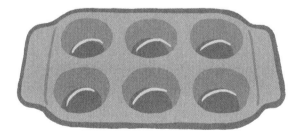

TOOLS FOR GRILLING

GRILLING is cooking food over high, direct heat and with air circulation (like the grates on a grill or a grill pan). Grilling, even with a gas grill or in a grill pan, adds a lot of charred flavor, and it's great for eking flavor out of tender vegetables and lean proteins. Think zucchini, onions, chicken breast, and filet mignon. Recommended tools:

- **grill:** gas is easiest, charcoal has a more natural flavor, and wood chips are only for the adventurous who want to be a genius about grilling . . . which could be you. Choose your own adventure. Please grill outside, thank you, and goodnight.
- **grill pan:** perfectly fine on a stove with a healthy exhaust fan, unless you want to set off your fire alarm (which you can do and then just comfort your dog or child after you turn it off)
- **sheet pan:** to be used in the oven broiler to mimic "upside-down" grilling, which isn't always ideal, since many oven broilers do not have a good attitude about life
- **long-handled tongs and spatula:** if you use a grill, your hands will be grateful

TOOLS FOR SAUTÉING

SAUTÉING is cooking food with any level of direct heat, often food that's cut into smaller pieces. Think making a stir-fry, browning ground beef, sautéing fresh green beans in hot olive oil and lemon juice, and sizzling diced onions and carrots in butter as the base for a soup.

Recommended tools:

- **skillet, maybe multiple:** cast iron is great for meat and potatoes but not for tomatoes or anything with a lot of liquid. A nonstick skillet is great for (wait for it) keeping foods from sticking but not great for getting a crispy sear on a steak. Stainless steel holds its heat and helps get a great color on foods, but it can be a bear to clean up because of all the sticking. Most people have a couple of options in their cabinets. (Side note: this is why cookware sets often don't work; you might want stainless steel saucepans but not skillets. Very few materials work for all cooking techniques equally well.)
- **saucepan or Dutch oven:** the high sides don't allow as much heat circulation, which means your food likely won't get as crispy

TOOLS FOR STEAMING

STEAMING is cooking food with contained, moist heat, with tenderness being the goal. Steaming also doesn't involve direct heat or fat, so it's the least flavorful of ways to cook food, especially if you use water and not chicken stock or wine. No shade to steaming. I'm just speaking truth.

Recommended tools:

- **saucepan with a lid**
- **metal steamer basket,** which fits inside a saucepan
- **bamboo steamer basket,** which is perched in a skillet above water
- **Instant Pot**

TOOLS FOR BRAISING, SOUPS, AND STEWS

BRAISING is cooking food in low, moist, direct heat. Think short ribs, a Sunday roast, or anything where liquid is present, but the food isn't fully submerged. Soups and stews use the same kind of heat but a lot more liquid.

Recommended tools:

- **Dutch oven:** for use on the stove or in the oven, since braising can involve either
- **Instant Pot:** for pressure cooking, which is basically braising at warp speed
- **slow cooker:** a "set it and forget it" form of braising but with less control over the fat and heat—that is, the flavor

TOOLS FOR COOKING PASTA, RICE, AND GRAINS

STEAMING is cooking the grain or pasta in just enough water for the grain to soak it up until tender. There's no remaining water when the grain or pasta is tender and done.

BOILING is cooking the grain or pasta in a full pot of water, then draining the water off once the food is tender.

Recommended tools:

- **saucepan or large pot:** a lid is necessary for steaming but not for boiling, and some people like glass lids so they can see if the food looks done without lifting the lid and losing the heat
- **Instant Pot:** more for steaming than boiling, but there are recipes for Instant Pot pasta that work well
- **rice cooker:** my husband is Japanese and so is our rice cooker, but you can get any well-rated electric rice cooker online or in a kitchen supply store
- **sieve:** something to help you drain boiled foods, and a sieve or colander are both possibilities

Pro tip: If you make a lot of pasta, consider a big pot that's cheap and can go in the dishwasher. Not all cookware needs to be so high quality that it should be babied, especially when its primary task is boiling spaghetti.

How to Use Your Instant Pot

1. Know the basics.
An Instant Pot is a small appliance best known for being a pressure cooker but also is a slow cooker, rice cooker, and yogurt maker.

2. Know where it'll go.
It can be quite large. If you're thinking about buying one, no matter the size, imagine where you'll store it before you buy it. Otherwise, you'll bring one home, have nowhere in the kitchen to put it, and it'll be stored too far away for you to actually get any use out of it.

3. Know what it's good for.
Stews, braises, soups, large cuts of meat (pork shoulder, beef roast), steaming vegetables, dried beans, and grains. Any dish that is liquid and moist is great cooked in the Instant Pot.

4. Know what it's not good for.
Foods/recipes that are mostly sautéed, seared, or grilled. Food can't get crispy in the Instant Pot.

5. Understand the seal.
There's a rubber ring on the inside of the lid. If that ring is not securely in place, the Instant Pot will not come to pressure and your food won't cook. You also must seal the valve to trap in the pressure. You turn the toggle on top of the lid to "sealing" when you begin cooking. When cooking is finished, if desired you can quick-release the pressure by carefully moving the toggle to "venting." Or you let the pressure release naturally and then open the lid.

6. Use the sauté function.
If you are making soup like a Lazy Genius or want some color on beef before turning it into a stew, there is a sauté function that can accomplish that for you without dirtying another pan. Just be sure to change the setting from sauté to pressure cook when it's time to seal the lid.

7. Essentialize your tools.
Many Instant Pot cookbooks and experts will recommend other useful tools that work in conjunction with the appliance, but as you already know, they are useful only if you use the pot. Don't invest in extra tools until you know you need them.

8. Essentialize your recipes.
If your Instant Pot can cook yogurt, that doesn't mean you have to use it for that. Only use it for recipes that make sense in your life right now. Just because something can doesn't mean it should.

9. Enjoy your own rhythm.
You can use the Instant Pot weekly, monthly when you're doing a batch of meal prep, or whenever you think about it. Just because someone else uses it more or less often than you do doesn't make your rhythm wrong.

10. Start small.
Pick one recipe or ingredient you've wanted to make using the Instant Pot. Make that one thing a few times and get the hang of it before moving on to something else. You don't have to learn all the functions and possibilities at once.

TOOLS FOR CUTTING AND BLENDING FOOD

- **chef's knife:** The all-purpose workhorse in your kitchen and one of the only things I will mildly boss you into getting. Go to a specialty kitchen store and hold some knives. That sounds aggressive, but it's worth it. If a knife feels good in your hand, you'll use it. If you're not in the market for a new knife, get the one you have professionally sharpened. It'll change your life.

- **paring knife:** These are the tiny knives that are great for cutting hulls off strawberries and taking the cores out of apple slices.

- **serrated knife:** This is the knife with a curvy sharp blade. Steak knives are serrated, and if you bake bread or buy from a bakery, a serrated knife will make your loaves so happy when slicing them.

- **kitchen shears:** You can chop herbs, cut string off a roast chicken, or open a stubborn box of Goldfish crackers with kitchen shears.

- **mandolin:** A mandolin looks like a tiny medieval torture device but it is used for slicing things so thin that they almost disappear. I personally am a wuss and afraid of losing a finger, so I have stayed off the mandolin train, although I'm sure it's very nice there.

- **box grater:** Just one of the ways to grate stuff, but a solid pick to be sure. Just watch your fingers.

- **Microplane:** These little guys are the tiniest graters ever. Great for hard cheeses like Parmesan and Romano, as well as getting the zest from lemons and limes.

- **food processor:** You can use this to blend and grate, depending on the attachments included.

- **immersion blender:** This is basically a portable blender that you can stick into a pot of something and make it smooth. Most aren't as strong as stand blenders, but that might not matter depending on what you personally need in your kitchen.

- **stand blender:** This guy is likely worth the space it takes up if you make a lot of smoothies, creamy blended soups, your own almond milk, or frozen margaritas.

- **vegetable peeler:** I will be an evangelist for the Swiss peeler, which has the blade perpendicular to the handle. The movement is so much easier on my wrist, but you do you.

- **cutting board:** Your knives need a friend, a surface to rely on. Wood and plastic are the most common material choices, plastic being the best for raw meat since it can go in the dishwasher.

A Case for Wooden Cutting Boards

1. A wooden board is beautiful. Even covered in food, it's so very pretty.

2. A wooden board is kinder to your knives. Wood preserves the sharpness of your knives for a lot longer than if you cut on plastic or (gulp) glass.

3. A wooden board is easy to clean. Unless you are cutting meat (which is the one time I don't recommend using wood—see point 7), most days you can wipe the board with a damp rag and call it a day. If the board has acquired an odor, rub a little salt into the board with the cut side of a lemon. You can also use fresh lemon juice and a scrub brush. Both ways disinfect, loosen any food bits, and make the board smell good. *Do not put a wooden board in the dishwasher or soak it in water.*

4. A wooden board stays put. Many plastic boards get a little antsy on the counter, but wooden boards are sturdy, dependable, and again very beautiful. They're basically the kitchen-tool version of Poldark.

5. A wooden board lasts forever. If you treat it with butcher block oil maybe once a year, you'll be fine. It's not like caring for a puppy.

6. A wooden board can also be a serving platter. I trust that we are all still on board with charcuterie boards around here. Your wooden board can be used for that purpose, for serving pie or cookies, for heaping up toppings for a taco bar, or for anything else that needs a serving surface.

7. A wooden board doesn't have to be your only board. In fact, it shouldn't be. Because wooden boards are porous, those meat juices will get down in there and never get out again. Have a plastic or composite wood board that is dishwasher safe for any raw meat preparation.

Thank you for embarking with me on this wooden board journey.

Lazy Genius Knife Skills

Most every food gets cut in this order: slice, stick, dice.

- **slice:** You cut slices of varying widths from a whole. A sliced onion looks like a cross-section of an onion. A sliced piece of bread is cut from the whole loaf. A slice of turkey comes off the whole turkey breast. Basically, when slicing something, the knife goes through the item one time.

- **stick:** A stick is made by taking a slice and then cutting it into strips. Think french fries, carrot sticks, and bell peppers that you dip in ranch dressing. This is often called a julienne, but for years I thought it was someone's name and not how to cut a vegetable.

- **dice:** Think of dice as a small cube, and in order to get to the cube, you have to break the whole down into smaller and smaller parts. For example, if you need to dice a potato, you cut it into even slices, then cut those slices into sticks, and finally cut those sticks into dice. Hello, tiny squares.

- **chunk:** These are basically what I call massive dice. Think big vegetable chunks for skewers or beef stew. You can still break them down to dice; they're just in way bigger slices, sticks, and chunks.

- **chop:** Chopping is the Wild West. It's making lots and lots of cuts to have something really small and the action has very little precision to it. Put your non-cutting hand on top of the tip of the knife for leverage, and then rock the knife back and forth across the food.

- **grate:** This is when you rub a food along a rough surface to create tiny pieces, like grated cheese for pasta, or grated potatoes for hash browns. (I'm not trying to grate-splain you, but you might not know and feel super embarrassed to ask.)

- **peel:** You take the outer layer off something.

- **blend:** I sometimes forget that blending is just cutting stuff up at top speed, and you might need to do that in your kitchen, especially if you're a sauce or creamy soup person.

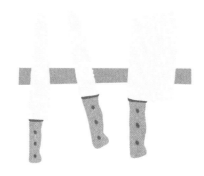

TOOLS FOR MOVING FOOD AROUND AND HOW TO DO IT

These are the tools you *could* use. You get to decide.

- **wooden spoon:** This is my favorite tool for stirring. Wooden spoons don't scratch your pans, they feel good in your hand, and they're sturdy and beautiful.

- **large, deep spoon:** Here's your dishing requirement. If you want to serve mashed potatoes, casseroles, and fruit salad in less time than it took you to make the thing, use a large, deep spoon. When dishing out, try to match the shape of the tool to the shape of the vessel you're taking food out of; for example, a spatula is great when serving from a sheet pan, while a round spoon is better from a saucepan. Any material is fine, but I prefer plastic or silicone because the sound of metal on metal makes me retreat into my own soul.

- **slotted spoon:** This is only if you've steamed or boiled food that needs to be separated from its liquid in order to be dished. Think warmed canned vegetables.

- **spider:** This is like a large slotted spoon but made of metal and with bigger holes to filter out hot oil, often used during deep-frying.

- **ladle:** If you make soup, a ladle is a game-changer. A coffee mug or large spoon will work, but isn't as efficient and is likely a bit messier, too.

- **tongs:** Perfect for lifting, tossing, and certain kinds of flipping (think chicken, not pancakes). Tongs are the best tool for tossing jobs, across the board. Two large, flat spoons or forks are second best.

- **spatula:** There are many kinds to choose from, but spatulas (or turners) are your all-purpose flippers. The more tender the food (pancakes), the thinner the spatula should be. Metal is important for a grill; plastic is likely fine everywhere else. I also like to have a spatula with holes and one without; the one without is for certain kinds of serving.

- **silicone spatula:** These in various sizes are what you want for emptying containers. Getting pancake batter out of the bowl, pumpkin puree out of the can, and mustard from the jar are tasks all highly improved with a silicone spatula. I like mine sturdy and not super flexible, kind of like me.

- **bench scraper:** This is my secret weapon in the kitchen. It's great for transporting a food item from one location to the next, but it's also great for cutting bread and cookies, cubing butter, and scraping off counters, tables, and underneath kitchen tables when you discover the garden of dried rice your toddler left behind.

- **whisk:** This is obviously your tool for whisking and also perhaps for mixing, depending on the situation. Balloon whisks (the ones that look like a ball) are the most common and easy to use. Flat whisks are fine and best for whisking pan sauces, if that's your thing. If it's not, skip it.

- **hand or stand mixer:** Obviously, if you do a lot of mixing, you might be glad you have either a hand or a stand mixer. But if you don't bake, make mashed potatoes, or do anything that requires a mixer, you don't have to have one, especially when they take up decent real estate in your kitchen.

You think I'm kidding, but so many people aren't sure what tool to use for what task. Now you know.

And these are the ways you move food around.

- **stir:** You're just keeping things moving, keeping them from burning, maybe turning two things into one, making lots of circular movements.

- **flip:** You've cooked one side. Now you need to cook the other side.

list continues >>

- **mix:** This is when multiple things turn into one thing. Salad dressings, sauces, cookie dough, etc.
- **toss:** You have food that needs to be mixed but not fully combined. Think salads and dressing, spaghetti and sauce.
- **whisk:** Whisking adds air to a liquid, making it light and fluffy. Think turning cream into whipped cream and egg whites into meringue. Whisking is also a way to cheat flour sifting.
- **dish:** Gossip. Kidding. Dishing is removing food from the pot or pan to its second location. Generally, the quicker you can do this, the happier the eaters.
- **lift:** This is dishing, but for entire whole things, like a steak, a piece of chicken, or a panini fresh off the press.
- **empty:** You want to get out every. last. drop.
- **transport:** If you chop onions on your wooden cutting board that I convinced you to buy, you need a way to transport them to wherever they're going. Your hands work fine. You might want a tool, though, such as a bench scraper.
- **fold:** As in "fold in the cheese." This is when you use a spatula to slowly and gently mix two ingredients, often with different texture and thickness, to help preserve the temperature or the texture.
- **cut in:** This isn't about your fingers. Sometimes in biscuit or baking recipes, you're supposed to cut the butter into the flour. That just means you break the butter into small pieces while it's in the flour. The specialized tool for this is a pastry cutter, but a bench scraper or even a fork can work.

TOOLS FOR MEASURING

What you can measure:

- **dry ingredients:** flour, bread crumbs, spices, etc.
- **wet ingredients:** oil, vanilla, chicken stock, etc.
- **the temperature of food to see if it's ready:** the inside of a chicken, a loaf of bread, or a saucepan of sugar that's turning into caramel.

How to measure:

- **mixing cups and spoons:** It's the most common: the stacked ¼ to 1 cup measures and the teaspoons and tablespoons on a silver ring. Best for dry, fine for wet.
- **liquid measuring cups:** These are the glass measuring cups that have a spout. It's much easier to measure liquids without spilling and it tends to be a more accurate measurement than using regular mixing cups. These work as a vessel to whisk non-measured stuff, too, like bonus mixing bowls.
- **kitchen scale:** I love a kitchen scale to measure by weight instead of by volume, eliminating the need for a lot of extra measuring cups. Most scales measure by ounces and grams, and many models have a "zero" function whereby the weight restarts at zero when it's time to add the next thing. It keeps you from having to add in your head, which is always a bonus for me.
- **instant-read digital thermometer:** Chicken should be about 165°F when it's done. A loaf of bread is around 200°F. Sometimes it's nice to not have to guess.
- **clip-on thermometer:** Proper temperature is essential for both deep-frying and making candy, so unless you do one of those things, you can skip this type of thermometer.

TASKS
How to Keep Up with It All

Rule #1: Do just one morning thing the night before.

Make lunch, prep the coffee, choose your outfit, pack your laptop bag, sign the homework forms . . . do something that needs to happen tomorrow, tonight. Extra breakfast time might be worth the trade.

Rule #2: Choose easy foods.

Frozen Stuff

- **Sweet:** fully baked muffins, quick breads, pancakes, waffles, smoothie packs
- **Savory:** breakfast sandwiches, burritos, hash browns, quiche cups, precooked bacon

Prepped Stuff

- Overnight oatmeal, yogurt-granola parfaits, and hard-boiled eggs can be ready to go. Omelet or hash ingredients can be prepped and thrown into a skillet for a quick hot breakfast. (Washing a pan takes less than a minute; sometimes it's worth it. Sometimes.)

Pantry Stuff

- The usual suspects: cereal, Pop-Tarts, instant oatmeal, and protein bars

Rule #3: Make it a priority only if it matters.

If your stage of life does not include a cooked breakfast around the table with your people, that is okay. There is no moral superiority to eating breakfast as you would dinner. Be a genius about it only if it matters.

How to Plan Lunch

The three most common lunch challenges are **volume**, **decisions**, and **boredom**.

Knowing specifically why lunch is a challenge will help you focus your solutions. Don't waste energy fixing invisible problems.

Volume

If you pack a lot of lunches, make the same thing for everybody. Not everyone will have their preferences, but lunch doesn't have to be perfectly suited to every taste every day.

If you're eating at home, make lunches that have several servings from one effort: soup, baked pasta, or a giant sub sandwich cut into pieces rather than six individual sandwiches.

Decision-Making

If deciding what's for lunch *at lunch* is the problem, decide what lunch is at breakfast or even earlier. Another idea? Decide one lunch a week and eat that thing every day. Change it the next week. If the frustration is all about making another decision, make fewer decisions.

Boredom

If you care about variety for yourself or your kids, your lunch challenges are different from volume or decision-making. First, make sure your kids care about variety. Don't assume they're bored unless they tell you. Again, invisible problems.

Consider having a Meal Matrix for lunches whereby you have a general idea but can vary the details. Monday is a sandwich. Tuesday is soup. Wednesday is a green salad. Thursday is a grain salad. Friday is something hot with cheese and bread. You can also take this approach for an entire week at a time over the course of a month. Week one is salad, week two is soup, week three is rice bowls, week four is sandwiches, etc.

1. Don't panic.

Your brain has a panic mode, and when it's *in* panic mode, **your brain chooses survival over logic.** Take a few deep breaths so your brain knows you're not in actual danger. I'm serious.

2. Look at your list of Plan B meals on page 92.

Here's why it's better to have a written/typed list than one that's just in your head. If your brain is freaking out, it's going to have a hard time extracting that mental list. Also, no one else in your family can see what's in your head, so put those Plan B meals in writing.

You've made your list for such a time as this. Use it.

3. Choose and delegate.

Choose a Plan B meal you already have ingredients for. Don't carry your panic to the grocery store.

Once you choose, delegate tasks to anyone who is eating with you. Sally grates the cheese. Bobby sets the table. Johnny opens cans. Get all your 1950s children on board.

4. Be kind to yourself.

If the panic stays panicky, if the meal is gross, if everyone is yelling, *it doesn't change who you are as a person.*

If the panic turns to euphoria, if the meal is amazing, if dinner ends with trust falls, *it doesn't change who you are as a person.*

Your value doesn't come from how well you succeed or how dramatically you fail. **Your value is rooted in love, not lists.** Remember the love of your family, your friends, yourself, and the God who made you. Even if you don't believe in that last part, you still believe in love. So don't let a wonky meal or angry attitude or another trip to McDonald's get you down.

How to Plan a Month of Meals at Once

1. Choose your calendar.

I like a cheap monthly wall calendar that I use just for meals. You can use a digital calendar, your paper planner, a whiteboard, anything. The only thing necessary is that you have a calendar showing the whole month, whether its only purpose is for meals or you use it for everything.

2. Start with your schedule.

Do not plan meals chronologically. This is where you lose.

Start with what you know is happening—book club, soccer games, city council meetings, birthdays, etc. Mark those days with a star or symbol, or write down the actual event. The point is to know what days need a specific kind of meal.

3. Put easy meals on busy days and celebratory meals on special ones.

If you know you'll be home later than usual, choose a quick dinner. If it's Billy's birthday, choose his favorite meal. Begin your monthly meal plan by choosing specific meals for specific days that need extra attention.

4. Use a Meal Matrix, like the one on page 95.

Pizza Fridays. Taco Tuesdays. Breakfast for Dinner Sundays.

Use your own Meal Matrix to fill in any remaining blanks. Not every day needs to be in a Meal Matrix; our family only has two or three main ones. The point is to make your decisions easier by narrowing them down.

5. Fill in the rest from your Dinner Queue, like on page 95.

To fill any blanks remaining, choose meals you already know fit your season of life. Also, give yourself the freedom to leave some days blank or to fill in a flexible option. Planning to have hot dogs on a Saturday night is easy enough, but if you decide to eat at Grandma's, eat leftovers, or eat out, the hot dog plan can wait another day.

Know Your Freezer Meal Life Span

How long can your freezer feed you? How many meals can fit in the freezer, divided by the number of times you want to eat a freezer meal every month, equals how long your freezer can feed you. Or, if you like math equations, here you go:

Freezer capacity ÷ freezer meals desired = freezer Meal Life Span

If I want to eat a freezer meal four times a month and I have room for twenty meals, my Freezer Meal Life Span is five months. I can stock five months' worth of meals at a time.

If you want to eat from your freezer eight times a month and have room for ten meals, your Freezer Meal Life Span is 10 divided by 8, which is 1¼ months, so your freezer can feed you for five weeks before it needs to be stocked again.

The Five Rules of Freezer Cooking Sessions

Rule #1: Have a plan. Make your own or follow someone else's. Know if you're making full meals or meal kits (ready-to-go components), how long things take to make, and what appliances/oven will be running and when. Don't enter a freezer cooking spree without a plan, or you'll never do it again.

Rule #2: Think about thawing. Imagine how the meal will thaw, and package the foods accordingly. I like freezing soups and sauces flat in gallon freezer bags to speed up the thawing, but if you're putting yours directly into a slow cooker, that shape won't work.

Rule #3: Google it. If you're unsure if something can freeze, check on the internet.

Rule #4: Label like it's your job. You think you'll remember what something is. You won't.

Rule #5: Don't be a freezer hoarder. The point is to make food for you to use. Don't hoard it for "the right time."

How to Plan Freezer Meals

How to Prep Food

1. **Choose your time.** When do you have the energy and resources to be in the kitchen? Only you can answer that. Mornings, evenings, weekends, one two-hour chunk, seven five-minute chunks . . . name the amount of time and time of day that work for you.

2. **Choose your scope.** How much are you wanting to prep at once? If you only have fifteen minutes, don't expect to prep three complete meals. It still counts as food prep if you do only one thing.

3. **Choose your food.** What food are you prepping? Choose whatever will give you the biggest bang for your buck, depending on what matters most to you.

4. **Choose your method.** Are you just chopping, steaming/ roasting ingredients, or cooking meals to completion? Choose what appliances you might use, what tools/ supplies you might need, and be honest with what you plan to accomplish in the time and with the scope you've chosen.

5. **Choose your zones.** With multiple happenings, it's helpful to create zones. An Ingredient Zone, a Chopping Zone, a Cooling Zone, a Packing Zone, and, of course, a Dirty Dishes Zone. Plug in any small appliances near the oven if you can to create a Cooking Zone.

6. **Choose your order.** List what you'll cook based on how long each thing will take. Whatever takes the longest goes first.

7. **Choose your adventure.** Do this with a friend or two and exchange meals at the end. Listen to an audiobook. Give your kids tasks and have them join in. Share a meal with a neighbor when you're done. Turn on your loudest Taylor Swift. Make it yours, and have fun.

First, you should designate a Dirty Dishes Zone (DDZ) and a Fridge Zone (FZ).

The DDZ is where all dirty dishes go until it's time to wash them. Pick a spot on the counter by the sink or the dishwasher, and don't put anything else in that zone, ever.

The FZ is a spot on your counter close to the fridge where everything waits until you put it all away at once.

1. **Clear the eating area.** Move the dishes to the DDZ, fridge stuff to the FZ, and put/throw everything else away.
2. **Clear the stove area.** Pack up leftovers, keep using your zones, put/throw everything else away.
3. **Clear the counters.** Same thing.
4. **Put away what's waiting in the Fridge Zone.**
5. **Load the dishwasher if you have one.** First, load items that have only one home—that is, plates and top-rack-only dishes. Next, load items from smallest to largest. Deal with silverware as it comes.
6. **Wipe down surfaces.** Fill a sink with soapy water if you have dishes to wash, or use your favorite rag and cleaner. Either way, wipe down all the cleared surfaces.
7. **Wash the dishes.** Wash the cleanest items first, and move from small to large.
8. **Wipe out the empty sink**.
9. **Sweep or vacuum the floor.**
10. **Celebrate**.

How to Clean Out the Fridge

1. **Gather your tools.** Get out the cleaner, rag, brush, bench scraper, a trash can, a cooler. And put on music with a beat.

2. **Take everything out.** Designate zones—questionable contents in Dirty Dishes Zone, Eat It Now Zone, Keep It Zone. Zones are for stuff that's obvious. Batch it.

3. **Wipe out the wetness and food debris.** Use a vacuum to get the bits, if you want. Soak up the wetness before adding cleaner.

4. **Soak stubborn stains.** Put a splash of hot water on dried stains and a rag on top to soften.

5. **Deal with the food on the counter while the cleaner works.** Keep, trash, immediately use.

6. **Wash the inside of the fridge.** Go back over it with a dry rag.

7. **Put everything back.** Wipe off the bottoms of bottles and jars before you put them back in.

28 Ready-to-Go Answers to the Magic Question (LGP #3)

What can you do now to make life in your kitchen easier later?
Here are some ideas.

Choose what's for dinner tonight.

Choose what's for dinner tomorrow.

Pull meat out of the freezer.

Chop an onion.

Fill a pot with water.

Mix a marinade or salad dressing.

Put the pasta and jar of sauce next to the stove.

Line a sheet pan with foil so it's ready for roasting.

Grate cheese.

Chop fruit.

Unload the dishwasher.

Clean up the dishes from breakfast.

Steam broccoli and carrots for a quicker stir-fry.

Marinate and freeze the chicken that's close to death.

Measure rice in the rice cooker.

Clean the mushrooms.

Wash the lettuce and wrap it in paper towels.

Make a quick tomato sauce.

Put all the vegetables you need on a cutting board.

Get the slow cooker out from the back of the cabinet.

Make cheese sandwiches to grill later in the day.

Cook bacon.

Cut carrots into sticks, dice, or coins.

Rinse and drain a can of beans.

Open all the cans you need for dinner.

Cut the onions and potatoes out of those red nets.

Chop herbs.

Set the table.

TIPS
How to Make Hard Stuff Easier

- Easy Tasks for Your Kids to Do in the Kitchen
- How to Never Run Out of Food at a Party
- How to Choose What Food to Serve at a Party
- How to Feed a Crowd
- How to Host Thanksgiving, including a recipe for Lazy Genius Thanksgiving Turkey

Easy Tasks for Your Kids to Do in the Kitchen

1. Press the buttons on the microwave.
2. Roll out/knead/crimp the pizza dough.
3. Fill pots with water.
4. Wash produce in a big bowl of water and dry with a towel.
5. Pour liquid ingredients from a pitcher into a LARGE pot or bowl, preferably close to the sink. Maybe even inside the sink.
6. Sift dry ingredients.
7. Mash foods (potatoes, avocado, etc.). Also, please don't assume they will actually eat the potato or avocado, because again . . . nonsense.
8. Dump seasonings into pots and pans.
9. Whisk stuff.
10. Crack eggs. Have them do it in a separate bowl so you can fish out the inevitable shell.
11. Add a pinch of salt to something.
12. Listen for the timer to go off.
13. Sprinkle cheese on pizza, burritos, pasta, etc.
14. Set and clear the table. Or at least parts of it. Maybe one plate. Pick your battles.
15. Unwrap things.
16. Put frozen cookie dough balls in a sheet pan to bake.
17. Rinse/cook rice in the rice cooker.
18. Wash or rinse dishes.
19. Put dishes in the Dirty Dishes Zone.

184 THE LAZY GENIUS KITCHEN

All you do is multiply. Calculators are very much allowed. Here are the magic formulas to remember:

Six bites per person per hour.
Three choices per ten people.

Let's pretend you're having twenty people over for a Christmas party that will last from 7:00 to 10:00 p.m. How much food do you make?

6 (bites) x 20 (people) x 3 (hours) ÷ 6 (choices) =
60 "bites" per item you're serving

Item one: sausage balls; you'll need 60. Item two: spinach dip; you'll need about 60 scoops' worth. Item three: cookies; this is tricky because it's about bites, not servings. A cookie could be anywhere from 2 to 6 bites. Divide accordingly.

Don't overthink it. The math always works. Unless you serve something wrapped in bacon; then double it. That's not a joke. Bacon transcends math.

How to Choose What Food to Serve at a Party

Choose multiple . . .

- Textures: smooth, cheesy, gooey, crunchy

- Temperatures: hot, cold, room temp

- Flavors: sweet, salty, spicy, earthy

- Weights: light and refreshing, heavy and rich

1. **Start with one dish you *know* you want to serve.** Maybe a party isn't a party without your grandmother's famous sausage dip . . . which is gooey, hot, spicy, and rich. Avoid serving another food that fits all those categories at the same time, and simply fill in the blanks!
2. **You don't have to make everything yourself.** Outsource. You don't have to be your own caterer.
3. **Make at least *half* ahead of time.** When your friends arrive, you don't want to be in the middle of a zillion things, stressed out, and then forced to disappear with a bottle of wine. Make it easy on yourself by choosing foods that can be made hours or even days before, or at least ready to simply pop into the oven when the time is right.

Decide Once (LGP #1)

Choose four go-to meals for feeding a crowd: two warm-weather, two cold-weather. Always serve one of those meals. Customizable elements are always great for a crowd.

- Breakfast for Dinner: bacon, breakfast casserole, muffins, fruit, etc.
- Greek Feast: grilled chicken, pita bread, tzatziki, marinated tomatoes and cucumbers, etc.
- Baked Potato Bar: russet and/or sweet potatoes with cheese, sour cream, scallions, rotisserie chicken, steamed chopped broccoli, salsa, avocado, roasted vegetables, etc.
- Taco Bar: braised pork shoulder or chicken, cheese, salsas, avocado, sour cream, beans, corn, roasted vegetables, lettuce, tomato, pickled onion, pickled jalapeño, lime, cilantro
- Baked Pasta Meal: baked spaghetti/ziti/lasagna, salad, bread
- Change Your Life Chicken (page 144)

Ask the Magic Question (LGP #3)

What can I do now to make feeding this crowd easier later?

- Prep food ahead of time
- Set up the napkin/plate area
- Pull out the trash can so folks know where it is without having to ask
- Run and unload the dishwasher so it's empty and available
- Run a sink of soapy water to soak/hide last-minute dishes
- Have a couple of answers to "How can I help?"
- Choose background music ahead of time and have it queued up

Go in the Right Order (LGP #11)

1. **Write down everything you need to do.** If you're making lasagna, list *assemble the lasagna, preheat the oven, put lasagna in the oven, pull lasagna out of the oven, etc.* Include everything. Details are how you don't lose your mind.
2. **Start with when foods need to be done.** If you want the lasagna to be ready at 6:15 p.m., you need to pull it out at 6:00 p.m., put it in the oven at 5:00 p.m., and preheat the oven by 4:45 p.m. so it's ready to go. Reverse-engineer your timings and create a timeline.
3. **Plug everything into its best place.** You might have an hour while the lasagna cooks. Decide if you want to make a salad, prep some garlic bread for the oven, set up the buffet area, or light some candles during that hour. Fill in the gaps.
4. **Add a 45-minute buffer.** The bigger the crowd, the more likely you'll need it.

Let People In (LGP #8)

Have the people you live with join in the effort. If you live alone, invite a friend to come early and help. People don't care so much about what they eat; they just want to be welcomed. Enjoy the fun connection that comes with feeding a crowd.

How to Host Thanksgiving

RULE #1: Remember why you're hosting.
Recipes will not save your Thanksgiving. *Why* you're gathering matters more. Do not lead with performance, being impressive, or being resentful because no one else will host. Frame your reason positively, and always lead with connection.

RULE #2: Know your weaknesses and ask for help.
If you're not social glue, ask a cousin who is to keep the conversation going. If you're not good at planning activities for kids, ask your Uncle Mike to do something fun with the cousins before the meal is ready. If you're not a confident cook, ask everyone to bring a dish to share.

RULE #3: Look for make-ahead recipes.
Do *not* make everything that day, unless being in the kitchen all day is part of your family's Thanksgiving Day culture. Otherwise, make some stuff ahead of time.

RULE #4: Pay attention to oven math.
The most stressful part of hosting Thanksgiving is getting everything ready to eat at the same time. If the turkey will be in the oven most of the day, choose sides that don't require oven time or that require very little once the turkey is out. You must do the oven math.

RULE #5: Start the meal with an empty dishwasher.
Clearing the mess of the meal will go so much quicker and leave plenty of time for football.

RULE #6: Plan out your serving dishes.
Make sure you have serving/cooking dishes for your entire menu. If you don't, go thrifting or borrow in advance.

RULE #7: Focus on light.
Candles, lamps, open windows. A room transforms with light, not just an overhead light.

RULE #8: Play music.
Music smooths the edges of awkward conversation and silence. It also makes people happy.

RULE #9: Buy disposable leftover containers.
It's so nice to pack leftovers and not worry about Aunt Susie needing to return your Tupperware.

RULE #10: Give yourself more time than you think you need.
Cooking for a crowd, especially on Thanksgiving, you will inevitably hit some bumps. Give yourself plenty of margin when you're planning your timings. Take a breath. It'll all be okay.

Lazy Genius Thanksgiving Turkey

INGREDIENTS

- a turkey, 10–12 pounds
- 1 stick (½ cup) really soft unsalted butter
- 1 tablespoon salt, plus extra as needed
- 2 teaspoons black pepper, freshly ground if you can, plus extra as needed
- 4 teaspoons of dried herbs (I use equal parts thyme and rosemary, but fennel and sage would be nice additions, too)
- 1 large white or yellow onion, peeled and cut into large wedges
- 2 large apples (any kind is fine) cut into large wedges, no need to peel or core

NOTE: If you're cooking a turkey more than 12 pounds, double the butter and seasonings.

Three Days Before: **Thaw the Turkey**

It takes almost three days in the fridge to fully thaw a 10-pound bird and five to six days for a 20-pound bird. PLAN ACCORDINGLY. No putting turkeys in the dryer.

The Day Before: **Season the Turkey**

1. In the morning, pull out the butter and let it sit on the counter pretty much all day.
2. Somewhere between lunch and going to bed, pull out everything you'll need: your roasting pan, the turkey, a bowl for mixing the butter, the wedged onion and apples, and extra salt and pepper in a separate bowl to use inside the bird.
3. In a small bowl, mix the butter with 1 tablespoon salt, 2 teaspoons pepper, and the dried herbs. It's heavily seasoned; don't be scared.
4. Take the turkey out of the wrapping, pat it dry with paper towels, remove the neck and the baggie of innards, and place the turkey on a large roasting pan or plastic cutting board with a groove to catch the juices.
5. Take a couple of big pinches of that extra salt and pepper, and heavily season the inside of the turkey. After you season the inside, stuff the apples and onion inside.
6. Take that seasoned butter and rub it all over the turkey, under the skin first and then on the outside. Top, bottom, sides—in every crevice you can find. Warning: the reason you want the

butter incredibly soft is that it will start to firm up as you rub it on the cold turkey. That's fine, and you're not doing anything wrong. Just keep massaging the butter into the bird like it's normal. If you run out of butter before you coat the outside fully, that's fine. Under the skin is more important.

7. Put the turkey in the roasting pan breast side up, cover it with foil, and pop it back in the fridge until the next day.

The Day Of: Cook the Turkey

Your turkey is ready to go in the oven just as it is, straight from the fridge.

Preheat the oven to 325°F. For a 10-pound turkey, cook for four hours. I like to keep the turkey covered with foil for the first three hours, and then remove the foil for the final hour to let the skin get really golden. Once the turkey is done, let it rest under the foil for about 20 minutes before carving.

How to Know When a Turkey Is Done

There are several methods:

1. **Use an instant-read thermometer.** This one is my favorite way because it's the most dependable. Stick the thermometer in the thickest part of the breast and look for 165°F.

2. **Rely on the pop-up thermometer.** A lot of turkeys come with a built-in thermometer that pops up when the turkey is done. Sometimes it's at the right time, and sometimes it takes the turkey a little far. This is my least favorite way because it's the most out of my control, and I don't want a dry turkey.

3. **Cut open the bird.** Poke the bottom of the turkey with a sharp knife and observe the juices that come out. If they're clear, you're all set. If they're pink, the turkey isn't done yet.

4. **Wiggle a leg.** Before the days of thermometers and pieces of plastic embedded in turkey flesh, folks would wiggle the turkey leg to test for doneness. If it wiggles really easily, you're probably good.

CONCLUSION

Enjoy It Like Never Before

Okay, pal, take a deep breath.

I know you're excited. I'm *thrilled* you're excited. I'm excited for you! Your life in the kitchen is about to change. That's worth being excited about!

But here's why I need you to still take that deep breath. If you busted through this entire book and are so pumped about the five steps, but still haven't put them into practice, you might spin out.

Don't spin out.

Hope is a beautiful thing, especially in the kitchen, and this book is full of hope. It's full of potential and promise and permission—and it *works*. But it'll work best if you go slowly and take it in small steps. You don't have to transform your kitchen all at once.

Start small. (LGP #2)

Small steps are easy. Easy steps are sustainable. Sustainable steps keep you moving.

You will experience your kitchen with more confidence and joy if you loosen up your expectations to fix the whole thing at once.

Remember how we talked about your kitchen's prep flow being like a river? Right now, you might be experiencing that river on a raft. Your current way of being in your kitchen looks a little janky, is often a rough ride, and you might have fallen off the raft once or twice, but you're still moving. Nothing is *wrong*. You just don't enjoy the ride as much as you'd like.

This book is your toolkit for slowly transforming that raft into a sleek canoe, maybe even equipped for white water. But you can do it slowly.

Apply one change at a time. Go in the order of the book, or pluck one thing that will make your ride feel smoother right away.

I imagine you sitting on the shore of the river, making camp at the end of another long day, and tweaking one little piece of your raft to prepare for tomorrow. You do another tweak the next night, and the next, and the next. Your raft slowly transforms into a boat as you learn from the ride.

And each day gets a little smoother.

You're not distracted by keeping yourself on your misshapen raft anymore, but you now have the space to look around at how beautiful the scenery is because you feel more secure in your newly fashioned boat.

It's *enjoyable*.

That's what happens when you seek to create a Lazy Genius kitchen. You enjoy being there more than you don't. It's not perfect, nor would you want it to be. Perfection is for robots. You're a human busting with laughter and compassion, spontaneity and peace.

That person doesn't need a perfect kitchen. She just needs a Lazy Genius one.

Deep breaths.

Go slow.

Have fun.

Enjoy your people.

Eat yummy food.

And be kind to yourself.

High five, pal.
You're doing great.

ACKNOWLEDGMENTS

As I think through the people who have made my life and this book better, it's almost embarrassing how good I have it.

First, to the Lazy Genius Collective. I know that a lot of writers say they have the best community on the internet, but they are wrong. *I* do. You guys are tremendous. Hope we get to keep doing this for a long time.

To Team LG—Leslie Fox, Leah Jarvis, and Letoya Monteith—y'all are the actual best humans to work with ever. I am so grateful for how you are so good at what you do, which gives me space to be good at what I do. May our solar system keep spinning for a long time.

To my agent, Lisa Jackson, thank you for listening to that Editing Weekend ramble when I was pacing the room and losing my mind. That feels like a great snapshot of our relationship, and I'm thankful for it.

To my editor, Susan Tjaden, you were the single reason I wanted to sign with WaterBrook, and that hasn't changed. Thank you for being great at your job and making what I do better.

To the design team, you made *The Lazy Genius Kitchen* the book of my dreams. Marysarah Quinn, I'm legitimately obsessed with you. Sarah Anne Horgan, thank you for loving Adam Driver as much as I do.

If you helped share this book with the world as a publicist, a marketer, a podcast host who invited me on as a guest, or a member of a launch team, or have done anything else that's currently unknown to

me because of the weird chronology of book publishing, thank you with my whole heart.

To Greg and Caroline Teselle, John and Emily Freeman, and Andraya Northrup for so generously lending me your spaces to write. Thank you, my friends. Your spaces truly feel like home.

To my accountant, my massage therapist, my counselor, my housecleaner, and all the amazing people who have shopped for and loaded my groceries, thank you for doing your work so beautifully so that I can do mine better.

To my masterminders Jamie Golden, Bri McKoy, and Laura Tremaine, you are everything. Thank you all for being smarter than anyone will ever know, for getting angry at me when I don't celebrate stuff, and for being such a safe place. I will take your secrets to my grave.

To my muse, Erin Moon, I love making stuff for you, sharing life with you, and learning about myself from you. Also, our children must eventually wed. In some combination. I am not picky.

To the internet, thank you for this new weird way to make friends and for these excellent people you've given me: Kelly Bandas, Andy Baxter, Chelsea Brennan, Courtney Cleveland, Adrienne Cooper, Scott Erickson, Natalie Hebert, Mattie James, Annie B. Jones, Sharon McMahon, Katie Moser, Bonnie Ohara, Anna Sale, and Kate Strickler.

To my fellow writing/podcasting friends,

thank you for making this job less lonely: Anne Bogel, Sarah Stewart Holland, Kristen Howerton, Shannan Martin, Knox McCoy, Tsh Oxenreider, Beth Silvers, and Myquillyn Smith.

To SGT, I painted my nails and then made a friend. You've been my biggest surprise of the last couple of years, and I love you and am glad you love me even though your unpainted pinky toe is cooler than my entire being.

To my local pals, you make me feel at home; whether we see each other once a day or once a year, you're why I love Greensboro: Diane, Ashley and Danny, John and Emily, Holden, Elizabeth and Seth, Jan, Kathryn, Andy and Brittany, Erienne, Griffin and Erin, Barrie, Anna, Daniel and Andraya, Nanette, Jon and Haven, Liz, Charlie, Hannah and Michael, and Alisa and Jason.

To Hannah Van Patter, I love who you are, how you've made me more of who I am, and how much you love the dirt. Seriously, it's like my favorite thing. I couldn't be more grateful to have you as a friend, and I hope we have many more years together.

To Emily P. Freeman, thank you for making me laugh, for understanding this pretend job better than anyone, for naming my stuff, and for holding my jokes and my

tears with equal reverence. I love you tons and tons.

To Hannah Kody, my seestra. I won the lottery getting you as my sister. You are the actual human best, and I love you so much. Everyone should have you as a sister. Every single ding-dang person. Except Luke, because that would be weird. Same for your kids. Never mind, this metaphor is crumbling, the point is you're exceptionally great. Love you, bye.

To my mom, Cindy Cage, people often seek out accomplishments so their parents will be proud of them. Thank you for giving me a life where I never had to worry about that. Your love for me is as strong and steady as it gets, and that means the world.

To the rest of my family: Jon, all the Adachis, the Tringalis, the Cage-Wilsons, the Kodys, and the extendeds near and far, thank you for your support and love.

To Sam, Ben, and Annie, I'm so deeply proud to be your mom, and I love you like crazy. Like CRAZY.

To Kaz, thank you for loving *me* like crazy. I am who I am because of you, and this book wouldn't exist in any form without you. You're the best guy, the best dad, and the worst joke-teller which kind of makes you the best. Always, always love you more.

THE KITCHEN CREW

An overwhelming round of applause to The Kitchen Crew for supporting the marketing efforts of *The Lazy Genius Kitchen*. You are the wind beneath our wings.

Amy Hanneke | Kelly P | Juliette Harris | Neva Hein | Jessica Turner | Amanda Murphy | Emily Lane | Nichole Middleton | Rebecca Lupnitz | Rosemary Soliz | Abby Irby | Grace Pratt | Kayla Snead | Christie Brewster | Alyssa Jennings | Ellen Morgan | Sally Caspers | Jennifer Abel | Karlea | Nick Deitmen | Emily Pious | Lacy B. Grant | Emma Bentley | Dianne Richey | Rachel McGeorge | Alisha Sadeski | Ashley Cook | Teresa Jaynes | Amy Stiner | Candice W | Shaunna Lyon | Kay Kerstens | Jamie Heinzen | Kristen Burnett | Betsy Prueter | Angie Schickerowski | Jessica Rogge | Caitlin Earle | Jeanette Downie | Amanda Gingrich | Jenina Roberts | Melissa Cooper | Kristin Fisher | Meggie Gilstrap | Shannon Barna | Meghan Smith | Giselle Orozco-Leon | Erica Miske | Elizabeth Marchant | Olga Bernhardt | Melissa McCall | Angie Fix Ortiz | Beth Van Gelder | Katie Webb | Sarah Kelly | Mary | Katie Spencer | Erin Westbrook | Alison Whitley | Samantha Conrad | Melissa Sheaks | Kristen Driscoll | Karen Shaw | Amanda Bryan | Ryan Leigh Runyon | Liza Clark | Kathleen Blake | Karalisa Sellers | Denni Heywood | Bethany Beighle | Sasha Catherine Burke | Sarah Belcher | Melissa Shafer | Ashley Hentges | Cathie Tingey Jones | Katie Goldberg | Sandy Flynn | Rachel Blalock | Heather Scholes | Brooke Wakeman | Katelyn Wu | Tabby Hamrick | Monica Andrews | Teri Deal | Jenn Davis | Casey von Stein | Jenna Dunseth | Emily Thoma | Alexis Birnbaum | Ali Anderson | Emma Redmon | Devon & Stacey Belser | Kyla Meilleur | Kendra Collins | Cheri Nixon | Melissa Irmen | Lindsay Livingston | Jessi Nicosia | Charlie Tyrrell | Tammy Blackburn | Amanda Graves | Amy Shinlever | Christa Gregg | Amy Bean | Ileana Bumbulici | Karli VonHerbulis | Kelli Finkenbinder | Allie Zani | Jen Payne | Alli Keele | Amanda Schuh | Julie Jarrard | Sarah Elizabeth Burns | Christi Conard | Kristin M Stephens | Mary Palmer | Staisha Momaney | Amber | Reba Cook | Kella Swift | Jori Maguire | Stephanie K Adams | Kate TerHaar | Mary Leigh Brown | Kristy Storms | Jill Pieper | Alexa Hogan | Megan Guilliams | Mofie | Erin Harley | Jaime Lee McHale | Grace Lewis | Debra Sim | Amanda L Miller | Anastasia Wolfe | Amy Duff Bonner | Jennifer Carter | Leslie Parsons | Hannah Allen | Janice Espinosa | Cindy Golden | Sarah Pifkin Ruger | Taylor Franklin | Sarah Bell @teachyourkidtocook | Robyn Hernandez | Jennifer Willerton | Monica Holmes | Stephanie M White | Melissa Hendrickson | Katelyn Geisler | Irina Scarlat | Stephanie Edwards | Lacy Parrish | Caroline Ives | Deanne Robertson | Faith Johnson | Chloe Langr | Melody Van Arragon | Erica DeWeber | Deidre Clack | Kelsey Shelly | Susan Epperson | Sarah Son | Sarah Traum | Liz Snyder | Rachel Mahoney | Lauren Ackermann | Julie Howard Kurzer | Libby Breland | Melanie Woodcock | JustPlainBeth | Theresa Diulus | Jessica Musick | Brigid Misselhorn | Narissa Kreutz | Mary Martin | Liz Spahn | Ashley Peden Bailey | Kelly Krause | Jennifer Cunio | Ronda Jones | Lisa Guimond | Carleen Jahnke | Lynn Eplawy | Bethany Davenport | Jessica Stern | Andrea Franko | Susan Davison | Kalindi Garvin | Sandy Vitrano | Chrissy Anderson | Michael Ann R. | Rachael Zimmerman | Bree Smith | Angela Park Tilley | Dahlia Hamza Constantine | Margy Quisenberry | Megan Birchette | E. Hannah Carter | grazi a. chiarelli | Jenn Collins | Brooke Robertson | Allison MH Murray | Mary Beth Eye | Sarah Meyer | Jackie Schrauger | Becky Fowler | Melissa Henningson | Cindy Bailey | Jeanne G | Hannah Zarbuck | Mindy Meyer | Caroline Sage | Kristy Stewart | Mary Rich | Carrie Hammer | April Poly | Laurel K. Moore | Jenn Mackin | Kristelle Larsen | Kara Keene | Laura Jones | Elizabeth H. Givler | Mariah | Amy Kepler | Jessica Driscoll | Stefanie Hunn | Anna Rubin | Jenni Brown | Melissa Goldstein | Josie Hill | Kate Mercurio | Daphne Jansen | Sara Kruger | Kara E | Suzanne Bissell | Brandi Rawls | Taylor Doran | Kaitlyn Van Dyke | Jennifer Killelea | Katie Jumper | Joy Steffen | Laura Mahoney | Andrea Underwood | Karen Elizabeth Ault | Michelle Briggs | piper john | Rebecca Arthur | Hannah Wessel | Courtney Tucker | Laurel Eshbach | Elyse Fulton | Gerry Lang | Kimberly Mulligan | Natali Evans | Sarah Worz | Leah Hockenberry | Lauren Forbidussi | Stephanie Wheatley | Donna Aufdemberge | Amy B. | Avery Elkins | Leslie Bitsas | Dillon Hendrick | Kirsten Muszynski | Nikki Turner | Lisa McLaughlin | Jeniene Diehl | Mandy Mendoza Gagliardi | Blake McGowan | Teresa Contini | Jessica Elizabeth Wilson | Meryll Kropac | Amy Franklin | Abby Akers | Chandra Apperson Hamilton | Kristen Joyce | Melanie Jones | Heather Bright | Jenn Paulsen | Mary Poquette | Erin Carter O'Brien | Shonda Knowlton | Amy Eid | Tara Pesta | Meghan Nichols | Courtney Cleveland | April Summers | Karen Bowman | Felicia Cottrell | Annette Hartman | Ashley Andersen | Mary Dehnert | Katie Patterson | Allie Buttarazzi | Courtney Dykes | Amy Beck | Catherine Wygal | Jasmyn Denton | Christine G. Walston | Meredith Bazzoli | Cassie Walek | Lezli Kuster | Shireen Goucluse | Mary Ann Livengood | Abby Winstead | Michaela Gillett | Wandainez Opitz | Joyce Clements | Cindy Fitzsimons | Katie Van Brunt | Anna McCall | Brianna Kay | Laura Kenlin Meiser | Kelly Alberts | Michaela Driscoll | Merry Jenkins | Karen Thornton | Ginger Huffman | Kristie Armstrong | Beth Rogers | Asheley Bumgardner | Marty Pittman | Ashley Strukel | Ashley Holzhauer | Tanya Paquet | Megan Looney | Cynda Pierce | Patty Berg | Ann Herlocher | Sarah Ward | Arianna Warrenfeltz | Sara Garcia | Peggy Collins | Lauren Puyear | Kristina Wait | Rylee Brazeal | Hanna Connor | Lyndsey Pohlmeier | Diana Alexander | Amy Coltrane | Christina Davidson | Lauren Drescher | Laura K Young | Katharine Dragner | Juliet P | Jennifer Haffey | René Beaubouef | Jennifer Dorman | Lisa Runge | The Planner Wire | Renee Piano Toomey | Jodi Hamilton | Ceilidh Harrison | Jen Knieriem | Rachel Kulcsar | Marija Crosson | Clarissa Heneghen | Georgia M. | Jen Campbell | Hilary Williams | Sarah Hutcheson | Melissa Biddlecomb | Kristen Kasmire | Lauren Eberle | Kalee Johnson | Patti Chisum | Sara LeBlanc | Savannah Richardson | Julie Colston | Katherine Killam | Ginny Hui | Donna Hetchler | Mollie Buckler | Megan McDonald | Melissa Lussier | Samantha Diane Hulbert | Alicia L. Reese | Sandy Grady | Julie Grubb | Holly Delgado de Matos | Hana Skinner | Ali Flannery | Catherincess | Lizzie Rice | Kori Marshall | Trish Sprain | Annette Silveira | Kay Schenkel | Kate Blakely | Prerna Sharma | Beth Rogers | Julie Dean Jones | Rebecca Hilton | Heather Weber | Jordanna Kearney | Michelle Owens | Steph Nelson | Sheila Racinez | Jennifer Helies | Emily Hensel | Erin Nolen | Jenna Kuhmann | Janelle Weethee | Nicole Lee | AnnMarie | Jessica L. Williams | Ali G | Beth Latshaw-Foti | Angi Morrison | Jamie Wuistinger | Shannon Wilder | Katy Bassett | Corinne Jessica Thompson | Annie M | Vicki Newendorp | Laurie Luplow | Nancy Burton | Cat Kessler | Bonnie Zimmerman | Mimi Butz | Jen Goding | Magen Hawkinson | Ann Pumphrey | Suzanne Cefola | Claire Ingram | Melissa Heard | Annie Johnson | Laura Loraine | Allie Bradford Brown | Holly Mosca | Gina M. | Jessica Fearn | Holly Burnside | Sarah StrakerDuncan | Kara Brutsche | Anna Kostopoulos Janusz | Brittany Danger Graham | Mary Aubrey | Katie Kornrumpf | Janice Schneekloth | Keisha Dawson | Rachel Bliese | Shelley Dodd | Stephanie Loux | Kaylan Keeler | Traci C | Sandy Bergeson | Eva Loraine | Bethany Douglas | Carrie Helton | Lucheluch | Melanie Cornelius | Amy Whited | Jill Haltigan | Angela Selken | Erica Hawker | Kim Zamolo | Carol Anne Wall | Megan Kreitzberg | Lesa Johnson | Mandy Cates | Sarah Black | Courtney Boone | Carolyn Hyslop | Jo Nygard Owens | Brenda Meier Kimaro | Lanne Thomas | Kelli Duhaney | Amber Richcreek | Samantha Lockhart | Sami Jo Carter | Erin Dickey | Leila Runyan | Kandice Kipp | Kellie Bornholdt | Melene Sexton | Beth Bender | Melinda Shaffer | Anne Savat | Daniela Vasquez | Colbe Galston | Laura Mikowski | Heather Messer | Kathleen Donahoe | Catherine Raynor | Natalie Guy | Samantha Boose | Kelly Norton | Amanda Soltoff | Erin Butler | Rikki Harry | Terri Lea Ikeda | Brittany Agin | Emily Tran | Kendra Langley | Marlea Hester | Karen L Magno | Lauren Williams | Jenny Tillay | Beth Ellis | Jennifer Allen | Tiffany R. Jenkins | Chelsie Timmins | Rachel L. Ross | Stacey Adams | Amanda Eklund | Natalia Smetanin | Suzanne | Kristen Ayotte | Nancy LaRoche | Laura Unrau | Kirstie Almy | Stephanie Jackson | Jenny Lynn Armstrong | Melissa Renner | Caitlin Mallery | Steph, Lorelei, and Vivian | NV | Megan Buehler | rhea magine | Nikki Lord | Debi Zahn | Sarah Lawhorn | Lindsay Harris | Victoria Lloyd | Elli Edwards | Crystal Stephens | Brittany Affeldt | Brittany White | Nella Smolinski | Bekah Harmon | Aimee B | Kaily Patterson-Coonis | Erin Beard | Emily Jayne Villhauer Lee | Becca Birkner | Amanda Michel | Tiffany Baker | Summer Sterling, Tavish Interiors | Fancy Jancey | Bethany Everson Na | Lindsey Bray | Beth English | Jayme Greene | Jessica Hammack | Catie S. | April Simpkins | Krista Alvarez | Kelsie Rose Gallagher | Stefanie Cortez | Heather Hamm | Meg Ledebuhr | Molly Householder Phennicie | Stacey Smith | Melissa Beichner | Sarah Diiorio | A. Steyn | Stephanie Hlavin Coen | Grace Chaisson | Lauren Burns | Adrienne Cooper | Andrea Mainville | Sara Parrott | Kalyne Stoltz | Emily Mencken | Amanda Wright | Catie Kale | Jacklyn Green | Becky Stevenson | Sarah Coleman | Laura Reu | Joy Kopcha | Rebekah Buchanan | Valerie Ramirez | Jody Gatewood | Ellie Goodman | Emily Roehm | Madison Gallahair | Kelsey Gillaspy | Carrie Kerley | Robin Walker | Kelsey Cody | Julia H. | Kate Gregory | Elizabeth Rank | Becky Armoto | Michele Leigh Davis | Jill Corona | Erin Buckles | Katie Tolksdorf | Jordan DiPippa | Elizabeth Hubler | Cynthia Falco | Jessica Hansen | Cynthia | Megan Ericson | emily mansfield | Rachel Baddorf | Chanel Sizemore | Anna M. Curby | Becca the Great | tammy carreiro | Donnalee Blankenship | Tabitha Parris | Catherine Farmer | Jamie Morris | Jessica Vick | Heather Mooney Williams | Val Crawford | Alit Braswell | Katie DeKoster | nfazio | Courtney Macri | Gwen Beattie | Megan Anderson | Lacie Van Orman | Hannah Pallotta | Jen Lepori | Amy Saunders | Lindsay Schneider | Elizabeth Homme | Courtney Hill | Sharon Harding | Angela Buikema | Jeanne Murawski | Jeannette Mullins | Hannah Gray | LeeAnn M. Christie | Tammy Sprecher | Tessa-Jean Tuttle | Fay Werner | Molly Hofker | Jen Bosen | Meagan "The Boss" Jensen | Lauren Niscavits | Renee Cool | Christie Johnson | Kelsey Wharton | Leah E. Ross | Amanda Linder | Misti Robinson | Megan Long | Rachel Dobrescu | Bethany Heindel | Leanna Nelson | Elyse Cullen | Kelly Fegley | Crystal Friedl | Sher Sutherland | Andrea

Bass | Jolene Joyce | Ashley Semberger | Andrea Staples | Emily lex | Paula Creech | Elly Widener | Jessica Eastman Stewart | Stacia Pew | Mama Jill | Joanna Kirtley | Rachael Roehmholdt | C.J.S. | Kirsten Robinson | Jenny | @sparks_of_curiosity | Kristin Brown | CiAnne Gresham | Mary Kate Dangler | Renee Meaux | Rachèle Ryan | Gianna Rae Kordatzky | Colleen Dougherty | Bonnie Chartrand | Ginger Newingham | Julie Salter | Molly Pendlebury | Megan Render | Tara O'Brien | Lizzie Wright | Holly Smith Webster | Deana Young | Aundi Allen | Tamara Phillips | Jessica Knapp | Lindsay Prifogle | Michelle Sheler | Kimberly Mayes | Andrea Brown | Melissa Jenna Godsey | Sarah Stange | Sarah Amador | Jess Dang | Katie Roberts | Amanda Calabro | Lane DePue | Kara Murdock | Christa Tipton | Annalyse Martin | Mia Purdin | Diane Hidey | Samantha Wyatt | Rebecca Sherouse | Katy Standifer | Elizabeth Hyatt | Heather N. Guthrie | Michele York | Liz Baker | Michaela W. | Angie Jacobson | Erica Yamauchi | Katy Robison | Sarah Lewis | Adrienne Mullins | Jacki Saslow | Alex Beard | Lisa Bene | Caroline Maclaga | Celia McCormick | Sarah Beth Parker | Laura Reese | Rachel Ryan | Michelle Rasey | Nancy Crawford | Heidi Elmore | Jessie Brooks | Brittany Smith Bihl | Erica Sperduto | Sarah K | Lauren Thacker | Staci Eckhart Schoenfeldt | Rebecca Hawkins | Leah Finn | Lauren Riefenstahl | Leanna Bedard | Grace Loughhead | Lisa Burns | Erica & Kelsey of The Girl Next Door Podcast | Becca Thiele | Jennie Lu | Adrienne Stroud | Emma Hinkle | Megan Rath | Donna V. | Christina Clark | Hilary Jarratt | Tessa Marzulla | Margaret O'Hanley | Laura Schrimpf | Amy Snelgrove | Sharon Janesick | Jess Harrell | Sarah H. | TheChristaClark | Kailey Phillips | M. Mock | Danielle Hooker | Kirstin White | Shelly Wyramon | Dawn Bahr | Michelle Aynes | Kellian E. Tonetti | Natalie King Kirkman | kduffkorz | Susan Harrison | Chris Jordan | Heather Navarrette | Stacey Benton | Victoria Harder | Kimberly Schwartzberg | Tina Noel-Valdez | Mary Elizabeth Morse | Sarah Emily Floyd | Amy Pignatella Cain | Alyssa Osegard | Kat Asharya | Millicent Falk | Veronica Hummel | Lauren Davis | Melissa Paugh | Jordan Brantley | Ashley Conway | Lora Potter | Jelena Antonijevic | Leah Golland (LG/LG = kismet!) | Megan Stelzer | Kate Turke | Dana Woodward | Jennifer Pena | Suzy Hillegas | Becky Miller | Bethany Taft | Devon Lowery | Alisa Meadows | Brooke Cherry Reich | Nancy Walton | Heather Saxton | Allie Anderson | Kristin Hanks-Bents | Annette Knapp | Lindsay Walter | Carolyn Cary | Jenalee Bolen | Lisa Jervis | Jill Glessner | Elizabeth Erlich | Amy Dunham | Esther Cramer | Katie Dingman | Louise Nichols | M. Jeanette Singleton | Bizzy Bracken | Kristen Lumsden | Amy Kathleen Leslie | Katie Volcek | Jenn Schaefer | Sarah Luhrsen | Valerie McFarland | Kelly Jones | Christy Rice | Jennifer Hayes | Nat García | cdmadison | Clare Aslaner | Melissa | Terry Kovalchik | Colleen Derber | Jessica Claxton | Courtney Bishop | Mandi Holmes | Autumn Battaglia | Emily Drazen | Erica Pence | Sara Miller | Krystal Bickel | Mindy Quinn Cederquist | Jennifer Spears | Linda Fisher | Amanda Waggoner | Wendi Jenkins | Sara Reynolds | Jane Rattray | Kaylyn McAllister | Kasey Wendel | Emily Stricklin | Sara Kay Sutton | Kristen Borst | LesLee Bickford | Robin Eichmiller | Jessica Cann | Melanie J Morris | Amy Luna Knox | Jayme Mangus | Carole McAuliffe | Miranda Keck | Janet Houser | Coley Walker | Erin Mullins | Christie Kline | Bella Bahari | Kelsey Rickert | TinaLou W. | Jenn Molinar | Marisa Surace | Christy Gutt | Taryn Wood | Jess Sawyer | Hot Mayonnaise Pie | Robin Walsh | Erika Smith | Jacquie Davidson | Luella Brown | Allison Crossley | Meghan Francis | Abby Henry | Angie Murdock | Wendy Warden | Anonymous Genius | Kristen Miller | Cat Weltman | Holly Tripp | Susan Carter | Amanda Roth | Rhyan Kwiatek | Erin Stoll (Style Thief Fashion) | Sarah Clark | Lori Ramsay | Jennifer Huffman | Ali Lavender Fox | Alissa G. Williams | Beth Bedell | Laurie Arcadi | Lisa Sexton | Laura Corcoran | Melissa McHardy | Jenn Murry | Nicole Clark | Tai James | Melissa H. | Shelly Voss-Carlson | Beth Burson | Kendra Evans | Joanna Martin | Christine Fritz | Jordan J Smith | Sarah Fettig | Melissa Sutliff | Daphne Stewart | Brandi Blaylock | Emily Marie Harpel | Holly Trafelet | Amy Hill | Alicia Barmetter | Kim Fuga | Andra Keathley | Kristin Valvano | Rachel Paeth | Shannon Schaefer | Chelsea Holmes | AJ Sanders | Andrea Maddalena Marshall | Carolyn Plou Rodriguez | Kaitlyn Kersten | Chloe C. | Taryn Shuler | Jennifer Hubner | The Beth | Aimee M. Peterson | Kim Aldridge | Sarah Hadley | René Graves | Jess Agee | Shannon Carrillo | Betsy from The Burnt Salad | Kate Matthews | Kara Leyerle | Ashley McCartt | Ashley Kay Mills | Jen Randall | Emma M. Hawes | Kylie Weaver | Laura Anderson | Lindsey Martin | Katie Martin Yoder | Jennifer Asmus | Candace Escobar | Shelly Blake | Laken Strum | Joy Cox | Mindy Collins | Eden Lowry | Becky Kalish | Nikki Kegerreis Scott | Catelin Drey | Erin Howell | Emilee Harborth | *Sally Woodruff* | Diane Egelston | Nicole Hawkins | Jennifer M Martin | Charlotte Wilson | Allison Manning | Caitlin Jowers | Amanda Gateley | Mia Toro Alsup | Dana Fischer | Natalie Schofield | Hannah Ruth | Terri Musser | Musical Mama Sischo | Abby Howe | Ana Glass | Rebecca Constant | Sarah Settle | Glenalyn Hunt | Kristin Esser | Cynthia Heredia | Amy Abell | Jennifer Pierce | Jessica Burkholder | Jen McCalmont | Elizabeth Longo | Kristi Henson | Jenny Kucharek | Sydney J Williams | Darcie F | Colleen Dunn | Ellie Brown | Melissa Lynnes | Chelsey Miller | Heidi Muller | Lyndsey Carson | Elizabeth Blount | Jenna Vickers | Elizabeth Baker | Kimberly Ravlich | Liz Aurilio Fenton | Diana Daugherty | Muriel Nielson | Beth Johnson | Thea DeLoreto | Grayson Daniels | Brianne Mejia | Meghan Kirk | Joanne Torcivia | Jaclyn Elwell | Stephanie Bills | Erienne Jones | Stacy Euphoria Laue | Julie Garza | April Hughes

| Gabrielle Miller | Carrie Dorna | Megan S. | Catherine Latham | Sarabeth Lewis | Lauren Honeycutt | Lolo McClure | Georgi Wilson Barker | Rebecca Mann Rayborn | Carrie Roden | April Butcher | Kassie Sweeney | Stephanie Wood | Lisa King | The Bixler Crew | Kim Holliday | Ali Pimentel | Tiffany Lingg | Kristy Hughes | Steph Novak | Vivian Levy | Robyn Gray | Jennifer Gustavus | Shelley E Hancock | Kristi Nickodem | Sarah Oldberg | Deidra Riggs | Tammy Skipper | Jamie Hutchison | Ryan Hester | Kristen Sieber | Nadine M Korab | Jamie Teagle | Beth Ann Roark | Tiffany Terry | Katy Burge | Meghann Kanapilly | Allison Cox | Anna Boechler | Katie McKenzie | Alix Ambriz | Emily Hawthorne | Danita Hiles | Sarah Williamson | Alex Shapiro | Kassie Austin | Brandyn Correa | Tricia Clarke | Taina Nixon | Heather MacIver Arnold | Bethany Specht | Megan Chavez | Amanda Clark | Katie Patton | Tamura Miguel | Sarah Smith | Kelly Gathman | Kaitlin Holland | Jen Digney | Paige Berry | Kimberly Shook | Hannah Taylor | April Burgess | Krissa Splittstoesser | Erin Murphy | Elizabeth Howard | Alison Spink | Krys Slovacek | Just Me | Amy Seelye | Mandy R. Schultz | Alyssa Grant | Hannah Griffith | Amy Romney | Sarah Denning | Ann Guthrie | Amy Gannaway | Bethany Anderson | Chelsi Holbrook | Andrea Shirey | Olivia Anderson | Julie Brizard | Claire Barham | Nikki Zimmerman | Stephanie Shattuck | Austin B. Rivas | Brittany Midyette | Lydia Fry | Colleen Wheeler | Andrea Gzz de Julián | Sara Eggleston | Bailey King | Jamie B. Golden | Laura Kohler | Laura Ridderman | Elisa Muñoz | James McAvoy | Ashley Fong | Rebekah Sherwood | Lorrie Tom | Carissa Surber | Amy Garcia | Caroline Grace Jones | Katie Frost | Kate Hagen | Candace Stimmel | Melissa Easterling | Marci Burger | Carissa Davis | Beth Vos | Megan Lorenzen | Megan Oliveira | Jennifer Fensley | Tracy Wilson | Kathryn Paxton | Becca Totzke | Bryn | Julie Cummins | Andrea Horn | Kelsey Salsbery | Sabrina Pursley | Abigail L. Smith | Lauren Iannatto | Jessica Chesbrough | Melissa Moorman | Jessica Dutcher | Jennifer Syed | Carrie Kim | Leigh Staub | Kristen Rue | Jess Burkett | Korey Ann Chambers | Tracy Rindal | Kelly Branch | Samantha Cassandra | Meghan Slocum | Madison Crandall | Kathy Larson | Beka D | Bailee Wilkins | Amy Hoffman | Leah Kruidhof | Alana Harrison | Erin A. Gillespie | Mary Wang | Lauren Huisman | A true believer | Deb Nodiff | Sabrina Jones | Heather Ward | Auburn | Brittany Schell | Heather Hurt | Sedonia Yoshida | Kaitlyn DeYoung | Lettie Burwell | Anne Bogel | Kristi Reaves | Christie Tidd | A. Brack | Sarah Bakun | Kelley Keller | April Kolman | Dana Dhom | Charissa Osborne | Caitlyn Kroboth | Blair F. | Christine Tucker | Cathy Cole | Susanna Bowers | Alisha Kawlewski | Julie Anderson | Sandra Renville | Ashley Holliday | Linsey Davis | Yvonne King | Cindy Edwards | Jennifer Andrzejczak | Jessie LouAllen | Mary Byker | Kylie Sommerville | Christina Bieniek | Chessie Leal | Angela Ernst | Alaina Gunn | Emily Blunt | Anja Christensen | Mona Thompson | Heather Bogaty | Sara Jo Flora | Olivia Sedlock | Erika Cardinale | Hallie Cooley | Caitlin Stauf | Jenny Williams | Rachel Hale | Jaimie Kostiuk | Whittington Black | Trudy | Mckenzie Monroe | Laura Bearden | Julie VanRoy | Jenny Lewis | Sarah St. Jean | Jill Ann Van Dolah | Hayden Dunn | Brittany Howell | Kate Dogs | Lisa Samanas | Kitty Kane Juarez | Ellen Linville | Laura Becher | K Wall | Megan Emilia Robinette | Anna Marinello | Amy Collette | Heather Willman | Lacey LeCroy | Beth Schulze | Erica Rawson | Sara Davis | Beth Kensinger | Maggie Noll | Ashley Hughey | Jennifer Vit | Amanda Libby | Christen Bevens | Sarah Beesley | Jen Gerdes | Kristen Gaffney | Tiffany deGruy | Sarah Ann | Julie M Smith | Emily Webb | Jacquie Harris | Melissa Paulsen | Jennifer McWethy | Jacqui Lom | Jamie Manangan | Cassie Papandrea | Anne Collins | Nicole Lugioyo | The Kendall Family | Myra Moran | Beth Kerbleski | Becca Anzalone | Gwen Tahmaseb | Katherine Alatorre | Amanda Regan | Melissa Maldonado Garcia | Katrina Helle | Sarah Schafer | Anna-Marie Murphy | Bailey Leitch | Jenna Culp | Molly Keener | Brittany Spotts | Jocelyn Van Hende | Amy Aiken | Malory Ford | Lisa J. Crowder | Kathy Rowland | Renee Nadal | Allison Tombros Korman | Calsie Oorebeek | Katie Gajdostik | Sarah H Kauffman | Melanie Lamden | Katie Wilson | Elizabeth Burnette Killen | Stacey Freitag | Elaine Bennett | Courtney Tallman | Suzanne E Jones | Mary Anne Maupin | Deborah L Williams | Lori Lentner Schwartz | Emily P. Freeman | Emily LeDuc | Shelly Storm | Kris Okazaki | Chelsy Montan | Rebecca Leos | Joshelyn Waite | Sarah Kitchen | Kathy Joyner | Melinda Tucker | Katie W | Ashley Black | Shelly Niehaus | Christy du Mée | Melissa Tulloch | Rachel Haney | Hailey Hennigan | Kelsey Blankenship | Dorothy Scifres | Caroline Osborne | Elizabeth Hightower | Jen Gorchow | Heidi DeWolf | Lisa R | Abbigail Kriebs | Meredith Jaeckel | Katherine Still | Emily Adams | Sophie Kusy | Natalia Dawe | Eileen Stender | Kendra K.Young | Graylin Porter | Jenny Bryant | Melissa Blue Sky | Lindsay M | Michele Tungett | Cindi Himple | Brooke Chehoski | Lauren A Coleman | Ali Jean Beatty | Angela Payne | Ariana Teachey | Roshni Neslage | Mary Jo Smith | Kimberly | Amber Romano | Gurita Narayan | Lynn Fagan | Emily Burr | Kristen Amann | Colette D Smith | Beth Watson | Rebecca Cochran | Stacey Potosnak | Amy Porter | Sara Peterson | Kara Carmody | Robin Marks | Abby W. Chaney | Kristi McNaron | Kathy Mallard | Sara Wutzke | Chelsey Headrick | Megan LeFaivre | N Hirchberg | Colleen Coppedge | Chella Tellez | Emily Cole | Abby Wingen | Katie Townley | Jessica Syswerda | Jessica J Forster | Sarah Buckner | Sanchez Family | Ashley Palmer | Jessica Precise | Hunter Douglas | fulori kirikiti | Kelli Galyean | Jennifer O'Gary | @imperfectlybeautifulus | Ashley Bowsher | Kathryn H | Colleen Roche | Stephanie Horlocker | Erin Miller Stephens | Gigi Sue | Kelly Dugan | Christie Viani | Rachel Blanke | Lynn Morejon | Abby Damron | Sherri Puzey | Michelle Murray | Jen Murphy | Tanya E. Crockett | Melanie Clark | Sarah Rykwalder | Stephanie Dawson Everett | Carolyn Lynch Munson | Kim Corns | Melissa Freeman | Shannon Olson | Rebecca Reid | Phoebe Clarice Wyatt | Jen O'Neill | Julie Ivey | Stephanie Jaczko Robinson | Steph Marburger | Brianna Woelmer | Melissa Marlin | Dava Renee White | Emily Jean | Meg Bucholz | J. McAuley | Alisha

Meador | Lauren Jochym | Stephanie Jones | Marissa Tenney | Maggie Penton | Kathleen Gimpel | Sue Steenson | Jessica Wang | Jill Dixon | Lindsey Catiller | Jennifer Allred | Caitlin Barton | Brooke Carpenter | Jane Worsham | Sarah-Jane Menefee | Hilary Kent | Jessica Standifer | Denise Cook | Melanie Cain | Jessica Buckley McCoy | Cali Callahan | Jenny Matthews | Sissy Silver | Nicole Franz | Shawna Palomino | Cheyenne Larson | San Diego Susan | Emily Snyder | Katie Taylor | Pamela Schreiner | Alaina Falk | Sara Taylor | Lauren F. Smith | Dani Cooper | Beth Keith | Rita Wong | Debbie Day | Michelle Panek | Fran May | Anna Carper | Anna Bulfin | Heather R @diveh2o | Tiffany McKeown | Hillary Sonnentag | Laura McClain-Biba | Nicole Dyck | Marla Medendorp | Susan Larson | Amity Blessman | Shannon Hoshauer | Ashley Vaccaro | Summer Burton | Michele Rowland | Jennifer Greene | Maggie McLeod | Tina Erickson | Taylor Laman | Kristin Lane Storment | Jen A. King | Sarah Frost | Hanna Maria Hixson | Jessica Holman | Sarah Riley | El Jefe | Rabiya Quazi | Gretchen Miller | Darcie Jenkins | Katie M. | Lynleigh Richwine | Denise Inda | Natalie B Walker | Kristen Laughlin | Lisa McCarthy | Miciah Lewis Baldrey | Karen Tompros | Sheila Garrett | Diana Clemow | DLackey | Dale Mandell | Tracey Johnson | Wendy Strader Steele | Jan Brier | Sonya Spillmann | Hannah Gunter | Lari Hall | Holly Marquez | Erin Mitchell | Karin Bloomquist | Andrea Dickie | Amy Adams | Haylie Johnson | Kristen Mullins | Laura Fairchild | Hannah Karner | Vanessa K | Melissa Pressley | Steph O. (from MD) | Patti Goins | Kathrin Sandall | Carri siebenmark | Regina Larzelere | Andrea Martin | Amanda Jaeger | Michelle Toohey (M2E) | Jill T. Brown | Jenna Wallace | Jennifer Lee | Michelle Shang | Melissa Parks | Nikki F | Peggy Leland | Rebecca Brouwer | Morgan Hollingsworth | Alyssa Berge | Dolores Cash | Amy Lacks | Jessie Moll | Allison O'Hagan | MonsterMomG | Ashley L. Potter | Veronica Herr | Kate Silton | Jess Edelstein | Jamie Fay Whitaker | Melissa Larson | Alexandra V. | Mariel Lee Schroeder | Aimee W. Smith | Merica Stum | Hope Keimig | Crista Bushman | Bec Jones | Faith N. Cracraft | Julie N | Holly Raulston | Meemamia | Jen Bower | Lynne Gentry | Summer Anderson | Michelle Stewart | Jennifer Ciraolo | Becky Skolak | Mardy Ortman | Meredith Williams | Janeal Schmidt | Karen H | Schuyler Zimmerman | Reid Fam | Pam Park | Brenda Campbell | Carolyn Catir | Gabrielle Stanley | Savannah Malia Cook | Laura R Smith | Beth Seufer Buss | Amanda Blackburn | Jen Durso | Kate | Kate Donnelly | Kori Rotondi | Meredith Draughn | Anne Turner | Chelsea Betterton | Kim Heuer | Suzanne Merrill | Amanda Bennett | Chrissy Palmerlee | Anna "Serendipimoose" Grist | Sherry Raviz | Heather Bothwell | Janet Carol Shantz | Rachel Kelsh | Taylor Etheridge | Beth Milano | Amanda Ovsenik | Ura Kondo | Melissa Thorson: Peachtree Enneagram | Sarah Burke | Suzie Starks | Lysa Peters | Leah McComb | Laura K Davis | Maghon Taylor | J Corman | Angie Simmons | Merry Rachel | Jenn Slowik | Anne with an E Turk | Emma Ashley | Sarah Chowning | Nikki Kosby | Jinny McCall | Dana Moore | Markela Parsons | Alison Dupee | Melissa Morales | Jennifer Lowe | Whitney Hannam | Sara Dixon | Mollie D | Alison Markley | Molly Snipes | Helen McLaughlin | Stasia Kroker | Emily Miller | .: Kara Gill :. | Deanna M. Jenkins | Jennifer James | Jen Keltner | Brooke Bigam | Emily Pehl | Andrea lea | Melanie Smalling | Maci James | Andi Mills | Maricela Wilkinson | Katie O'Connor | Michelle Shuman | Lori Snoots | Lee W. Cockrum | Cristina Dudley | The Korean Cowgirl | corina p. | Melissa Ribinskas | Lucy Grace | Cocina de Clark | Elizabeth Giger | Mary Elizabeth | Ashley Hernandez | Chelsey Hanna | Brandi Tooker | Naomi Newbold | Robin Brouwer | Amy Miller | Suzanne Davenport | Michelle B. | Kara Hofman | April Hardwick | Tricia Johnston | Brittany Moose | Donna Lynn | Robin Bothe | Crystal Miller | Kellyanne Engel | Lindsey Golik | Brittany A Walker | Merrill Skipworth | Mallory Eickhoff | Barb Cowles | Nora Goolsby | Kellee Johnson | Jennifer Guico | Jessica Herbel | Karalee Garber | Zoya Hoodlavitch | Alice D | Crystal Bilodeau

INDEX

NEW YORK TIMES BESTSELLER

THE LAZY GENIUS WAY

BY KENDRA ADACHI

**No more cobbling together life hacks and productivity
strategies from dozens of authors and still feeling tired.**

Instead, use thirteen Lazy Genius principles to create your
own system based on what matters to you. You don't need a
new list of things to do; you need a new way to see.

It's time for a book that has both system and soul,
and *The Lazy Genius Way* is it.

Available wherever books are sold.

THE LAZY GENIUS PODCAST
WITH KENDRA ADACHI

Being a person is hard, and The Lazy Genius Podcast is here to help you be a genius about the things that matter and lazy about the things that don't. From laundry to cooking chicken to making new friends, Kendra is here to welcome you into an easier way.

Listen to The Lazy Genius Podcast, in which she shares how to approach almost anything like a Lazy Genius.

Tune in at thelazygeniuscollective.com/lazy or subscribe using your favorite podcast app.

New episodes every Monday.

WANT MORE
LAZY GENIUS KITCHEN?

Same.

Join Kendra as she visits the kitchens of some of Instagram's favorite personalities and her closest friends to apply Lazy Genius principles in real time. And grab free practical resources online designed to help you get what you want out of the hardest working room in your home.

Find all the fun extras at thelazygeniuskitchen.com.

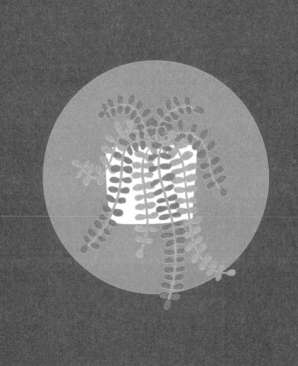